BOOK 2
CATAPULT
ENGLISH LANGUAGE

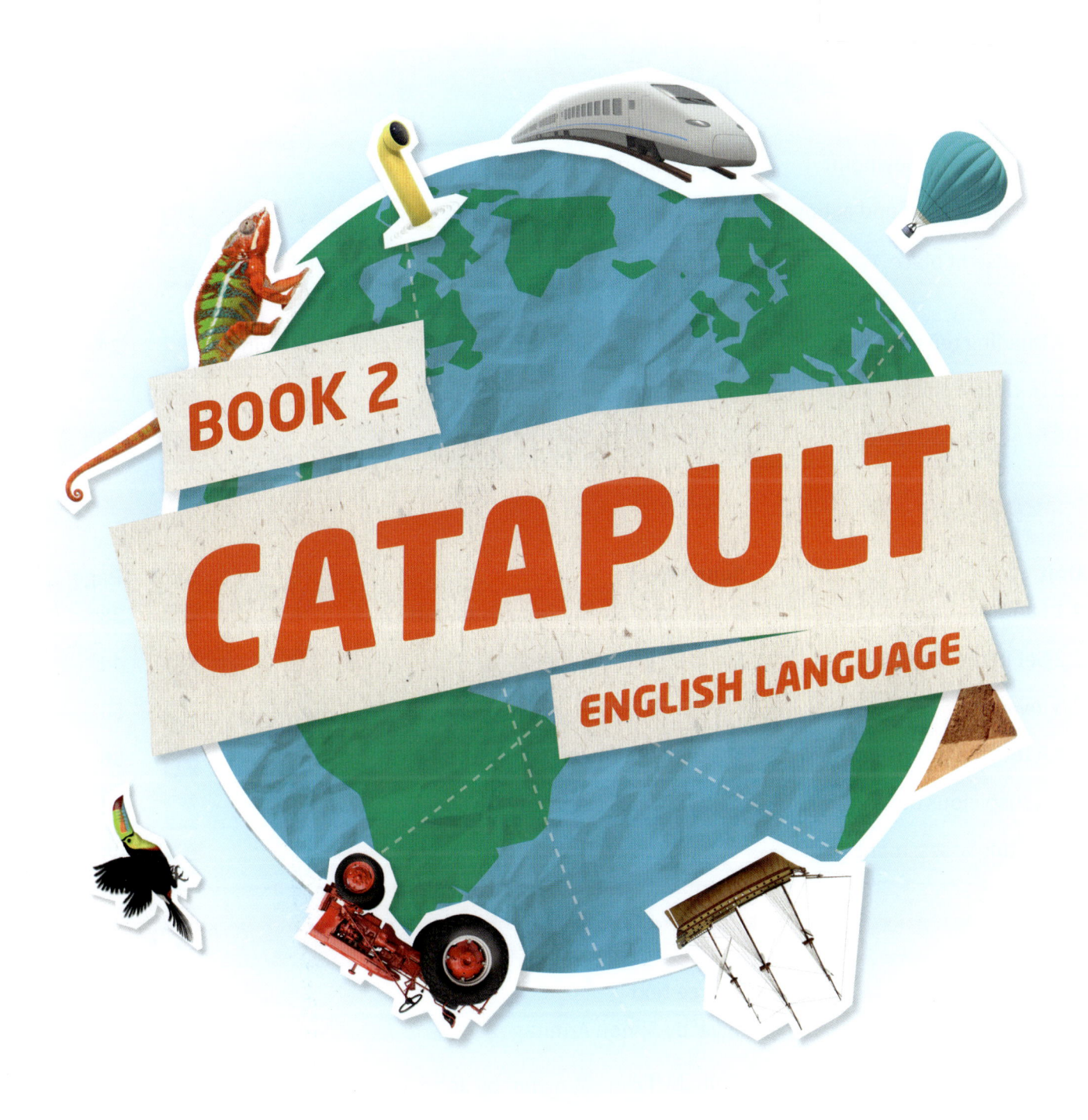

Christopher Edge • Peter Ellison • Esther Menon

OXFORD
UNIVERSITY PRESS

Contents

Introduction	4

✏️ Writing skills   📖 Reading skills

Chapter 1: Plot and pace — 6

Unit	Source text	Skill	Page
1.1 First-person viewpoint	*Once* by Morris Gleitzman	📖	6
1.2 Narrative pace and action	*Stormbreaker* by Anthony Horowitz	✏️	12
1.3 A sense of place	*The Island at the End of Everything* by Kiran Millwood Hargrave	📖	18
1.4 Building tension	'The Legend of Sleepy Hollow' by Washington Irving	✏️	24
1.5 Narrative shifts	*The Secret History* by Donna Tartt	📖	30
1.6 Reading assessment	*Life After Life* by Kate Atkinson	📖	36

Chapter 2: Genre and themes — 38

Unit	Source text	Skill	Page
2.1 Fantasy	*A Hat Full of Sky* by Terry Pratchett	✏️	38
2.2 Set in the past	*Smith* by Leon Garfield	📖	44
2.3 Invasion!	*The War of the Worlds* by H. G. Wells	✏️	50
2.4 A touch of horror	*The Sacrifice Box* by Martin Stewart	📖	56
2.5 A suspicious death	*The Christmas Card List* by Kate Ellis	✏️	62
2.6 Writing assessment		✏️	68

Chapter 3: People and voices — 70

Unit	Source text	Skill	Page
3.1 Different voices	'Give' by Simon Armitage	✏️	70
3.2 Serious comedy	'Crybaby Prime Minister' by John Agard	📖	76
3.3 Changing identity	'Old Tongue' by Jackie Kay	✏️	82
3.4 Persuasive voices	*Macbeth*, Act 1 Scene 7 by William Shakespeare	📖	88
3.5 Reading assessment	'A Child's Sleep' by Carol Ann Duffy	📖	94

Chapter 4: Autobiography and reflection — 96

Unit	Source text	Skill	Page
4.1 Unusual choices	*Akenfield* by Ronald Blythe	📖	96
4.2 Early goals	*Lord Sugar* by Charlie Burden	✏️	102
4.3 Overcoming problems	*Darcey Bussell CBE: Creative Successful Dyslexic* by Margaret Rooke	📖	108
4.4 Earning and spending	Autobiographical writing by Charles Dickens	✏️	114
4.5 Writing assessment		✏️	120

Chapter 5: Witnesses and reports — 122

Unit	Source text	Skill	Page
5.1 A terrifying experience	'Tsunami on Koh Phi Phi' by Laura Wales Holliday	✏️	122
5.2 Discovery!	*The Discovery of the Tomb of Tutankhamen* by Howard Carter and A. C. Mace	📖	128
5.3 Reporting the world	'A Remote Paradise Island Is Now a Plastic Junkyard', *The Atlantic*, 15 May 2017	✏️	134
5.4 Writing from the heart	*To Fight Alongside Friends: The First World War Diaries Of Charlie May*, edited by Gerry Harrison	📖	140
5.5 Reading assessment	*The Fire Outside my Window* by Sandra Millers Younger	📖	146

Chapter 6: Viewpoints and issues — 148

Unit	Source text	Skill	Page
6.1 Speaking my mind (1)	'Off With Stress' by Sgt Ellie Bloggs	📖	148
6.2 Speaking my mind (2)	A letter published in the *Western Mail*	📖	154
6.3 A call to action	'As parents we need to ask ourselves whether children really need their own smartphones' by Joanna Cates	✏️	160
6.4 A direct appeal	'Don't assume the only homeless people are those on the streets' by Polly Neate	📖	166
6.5 Writing assessment		✏️	172

Target word list — 174

Introduction

Catapult has been written to help students develop the skills, knowledge and confidence needed to make progress in English by providing them with:

- A wide range of engaging, high-quality texts dealing with some of the most important contemporary issues, adding to their general knowledge

- Sophisticated and useful vocabulary that they can incorporate into their writing straight away

- Approaches to enable them to comprehend more complex syntax, especially in 19th-century texts.

In *Catapult*, you will find texts from the 19th, 20th and 21st centuries, organised into chapters designed to build students' understanding of key aspects of fiction, as well as the range of non-fiction purposes and forms they are expected to study. You will find extracts from classic novels by H. G. Wells, as well as texts from acclaimed contemporary authors such as Terry Pratchett and Donna Tartt. In addition, a variety of non-fiction texts, including essays, biographies, diaries, blogs and letters, have been carefully selected to interest and engage students.

In each unit, there are clear links between reading and writing. Students are encouraged to apply new vocabulary immediately and use the texts as models to try out new writing techniques, with short exercises gradually building into more sustained pieces of writing.

Throughout *Catapult*, we have endeavoured to give students a sense of purpose and achievement. We want them to feel proud of their growing vocabulary and ability to read more challenging texts, as well as their increasing control of written language.

Built around core principles of building vocabulary, developing knowledge and understanding, and improving reading and writing skills, *Catapult* will ensure that these students are fully prepared for their future English studies.

Introduction

Catapult overview

Try	Apply	Consolidate
Student Books: students will try out new skills, broaden their knowledge and expand their vocabulary. Every unit of the Student Book includes: • A source text • A Word power activity • A Knowledge and understanding activity • Either a Reading skills or Writing skills activity • A Check your skills activity Every chapter finishes with either a Reading or Writing assessment.	**Kerboodle Digital Book plus Lessons, Resources and Assessment:** students will be able to apply the skills, knowledge and vocabulary they have practised in the Student Book. Every unit in Kerboodle includes: • An audio recording of the source text from the Student Book • An interactive comprehension quiz • A Word power worksheet • Either a Reading skills or Writing skills worksheet Both Student Books are available as Kerboodle Digital Books, and the resources above can be launched directly from the relevant pages.	**Workbooks:** students will consolidate everything they have learned. Every unit of the Student Book has a supporting Workbook unit, ideal for additional practice in class or for homework. Every Workbook unit includes: • A new source text • A range of Word power, Knowledge and understanding, Reading or Writing skills activities • A Check your skills activity

Plan

Teacher Books include guidance on delivering every unit, bringing together resources from the Student Book and Kerboodle. There are also short-, medium- and long-term plans, as well as answers for all the activities in the Student Book and Workbook.

Kerboodle provides a range of additional resources including spelling, punctuation and grammar interactive quizzes, editable versions of assessments, end-of-year assessments, mark schemes, skills-mapping grids and assessment levels.

Activity types within this Student Book

⚡ Word power	💡 Knowledge and understanding	📖 Reading skills	✏️ Writing skills	❗ Check your skills
Word power activities are based around the Target words highlighted blue in each source text. These words help to broaden students' vocabulary so they can then start to include them in their own work.	**Knowledge and understanding activities** help students to secure their contextual understanding and develop a broader range of topics to write about themselves.	**Reading skills activities** enable students to improve their reading stamina and increase their confidence when responding to less familiar text types.	**Writing skills activities** help students to generate ideas and write coherently for sustained periods, and to try out their new vocabulary and writing techniques.	**Check your skills activities** enable students to apply the skills they have developed in each unit in a more independent context to enable a review of progress.

5

1 Plot and pace

Unit 1

First-person viewpoint

In this unit, you will:

- Explore the use of the **present tense** and **first-person viewpoint** to build **tension**.
- Investigate how a writer's use of paragraphs contributes to **narrative pace**.
- Learn, understand and practise using new vocabulary.

The plot of a novel or short story is the events that happen in the story and the order these are presented in. If a story is told from a first-person viewpoint, these events are seen through the eyes of a character.

The narrative pace of a story is how quickly or slowly events unfold. Writers can control the narrative pace through their use of paragraphs and choice of sentences.

The extract on page 7 is from *Once* by Morris Gleitzman. Set in Poland in 1942, *Once* tells the story of Felix, a Jewish boy who believes that he's been left in an orphanage by his parents. Felix's parents are booksellers and when Felix sees Nazis burning the books from the orphanage library, he decides to escape to find his parents.

Key terms

first-person viewpoint where the narrator is a character in the story, usually the protagonist (main character), and the story is told from their viewpoint using 'I' and 'we'

narrative pace the speed at which the action of a story moves along

present tense used to describe things that are happening now

tension a feeling of unease or nervousness when we know that something important is about to happen

Unit 1: First-person viewpoint

Extract from *Once* by Morris Gleitzman
381 words

Once I walked as fast as I could towards the city to find Mum and Dad and I didn't let anything stop me.

Not until the fire.

I slow down, staring at the horizon.

The fire is miles away, but I can see flames clearly as they flicker in the darkness. They must be huge. If that's a pile of burning books, there must be millions.

I stop.

I wipe my glasses and try to see if any Nazis are over there. I can't. It's too far away to see people, let alone **arm bands**.

100 words

I can hear trucks, or cars though, and faint shouting voices.

Part of me wants to run away, just in case.

Another part of me wants to go closer. Mum and Dad might be there. This might be where all the Jewish book owners have been taken, so the Nazis can burn all their books in one big pile.

I go closer.

I don't want to stay on the road in case I bump into any Nazis who are running late, so I cut across some fields.

200 words

One of the fields has cabbages in it. As I get closer to the fire, the cabbages are starting to get warm. Some are starting to smell like they're cooking. But I don't stop to eat any.

I can see what's burning now.

It's not books, it's a house.

I still can't see any people, so I stuff the bread and water inside my shirt and take my hat off and pee on it and put it back on to keep my head from blistering and go even closer in case there are some people who need to be rescued. I wrote a story once about Mum and Dad rescuing an **ink salesman** from a burning house, so I know a bit about it.

300 words

Blinking from the heat and the glare, I reach the wire fence that separates the house from the fields. The wire is too hot to touch. I wriggle under it.

The lawn is covered with dead chickens. Poor things, they must be cooked. That's what I think until I see holes in them.

They've been shot.

The owners must have done it to put them out of their misery.

Then I see the owners.

Oh.

---

arm bands – when the Nazis invaded Poland, Jews were forced to wear a white armband with a blue six-sided star on it to identify themselves as Jews, while Nazi supporters wore armbands with swastikas

ink salesman – someone who sells ink for use in pens

1.1 Chapter 1: Plot and pace

⚡ Word power

Re-read the extract on page 7. Pay particular attention to the target words listed below. As you read, think about how each of the words helps to add to the impression of how close Felix is to the action.

Your target words for this section are:

- horizon
- flicker
- faint
- blistering
- separate

These target words have been highlighted in blue in the extract on page 7.

1. The horizon is the line where Earth seems to meet the sky. In the story, Felix can see the fire on the horizon. Does this give you the impression that the fire is near or far away?

2. 'Flicker' is a verb meaning to burn or shine unsteadily. Write a sentence, including the verb 'flicker', to describe someone using one of the following objects.

- a match
- a torch
- a lighter

The torch flickered and then went out, plunging me into darkness.

3. Look again at the following sentence where Felix describes what he can hear:

> 'I can hear trucks, or cars though, and faint shouting voices.'

a. Look up the word 'faint' in the Target word list on pages 174–175. Two definitions are given. Which do you think is the correct definition for the way 'faint' is used in this sentence?

b. What impression does this **adjective** give you of how close Felix is to the action?

Key term

adjective a word that describes a person, place, object or sound

8

Unit 1: First-person viewpoint

4 A blister is a swelling like a bubble on the skin, filled with watery liquid. As a verb, 'blistering' means producing a blister or blisters on the skin or on a surface. As an adjective, 'blistering' can mean very intense or severe, as in 'blistering heat'.

  a. Look again at where the word 'blistering' is used in the extract on page 7 and decide whether it has been used as a verb or an adjective.

  b. Write a couple of sentences describing someone getting close to a fire.
  - In the first sentence, use the word 'blistering' as an adjective.
  - In the second sentence, use the word 'blistering' as a verb.

  In your sentences try to give the reader a strong impression of the fierceness of the fire.

5
  a. As a verb, 'separate' means to make or keep things apart. Look again at the extract on page 7 and identify what separates the house from the fields.

  b. 'Separate' is one of the most commonly misspelled words in the English language, with some people incorrectly spelling the word as 'seperate' instead of 'separate'. One way to remember the correct spelling is to remember that 'separate' has 'a rat' in the middle.

sep + a   + e

Look at the following commonly misspelled words. Identify the part of the word that you think people might find tricky to spell and invent your own tips to help them remember the correct way to spell these words. The first one has been done for you.

achieve – 'i' before 'e'

successful

business

definitely

occasion

9

1.1 Chapter 1: Plot and pace

💡 Knowledge and understanding

Look back at the extract on page 7 and answer the following questions.

1. What does Felix think is causing the fire at first?

2. What impression do you get of the size of the fire? Pick out a detail that helps give you this impression.

3. Look again at the following extract:

   > 'Part of me wants to run away, just in case.
   > Another part of me wants to go closer.'

   Using what you have learned from the extract, explain why Felix has these different feelings.

4. Look again at the paragraph beginning:

   > 'I still can't see any people…'

   a. Someone who is resourceful is clever at finding ways of doing things. Find a detail from this paragraph that suggests Felix is resourceful. Explain your choice.

   b. What impression do you get of Felix from this paragraph? Pick out details from the text and explain how they give you this impression.

5. Look again at the ending of the extract on page 7. What do you think has happened to the owners of the house? Explain why you think this.

A fire can have devastating effects.

📖 Reading skills

1. Look again at the opening sentence of the source text.

   > 'Once I walked as fast as I could towards the city to find Mum and Dad and I didn't let anything stop me.'

   Why do you think Gleitzman has written this in the **past tense**?

2. Pick out the sentence where Gleitzman switches to writing in the present tense.

Key term

past tense used to describe things that have already happened

10

Unit 1: First-person viewpoint

3 As the story is written from a first-person viewpoint and in the present tense, the reader sees events through Felix's eyes and is able to share his thoughts and emotions on these as they are happening.

Copy and complete the following table to show how Felix's understanding of what is happening changes as he gets closer to the fire.

4 Now look at Gleitzman's use of paragraphs in this extract. Some paragraphs are very short, consisting of a single-clause sentence or sentence fragment, for example: *I stop.*

Do you think this speeds up or slows down the pace of the narrative? Give reasons for your choice, referring to different paragraphs from the extract.

Felix's perspective	What Felix thinks is happening	How Felix feels
'The fire is miles away, but I can see flames clearly as they flicker in the darkness.'	He thinks the Nazis are burning a huge pile of books.	He wants to run away, but also…
'I can see what's burning now. It's not books, it's a house.'		
'The lawn is covered with dead chickens.'		
'Then I see the owners. Oh.'		

! Check your skills

How does Gleitzman build tension (see page 6) in this extract? In your answer comment on:

- the use of the first-person viewpoint
- the choice of the present tense
- how paragraphs are used to control the narrative pace.

Remember to include brief quotations from the extract that you think are particularly effective in helping to build tension.

The Nazis burned many books, especially in university towns, in the 1930s.

11

1.2 **Chapter 1:** Plot and pace

Unit 2
Narrative pace and action

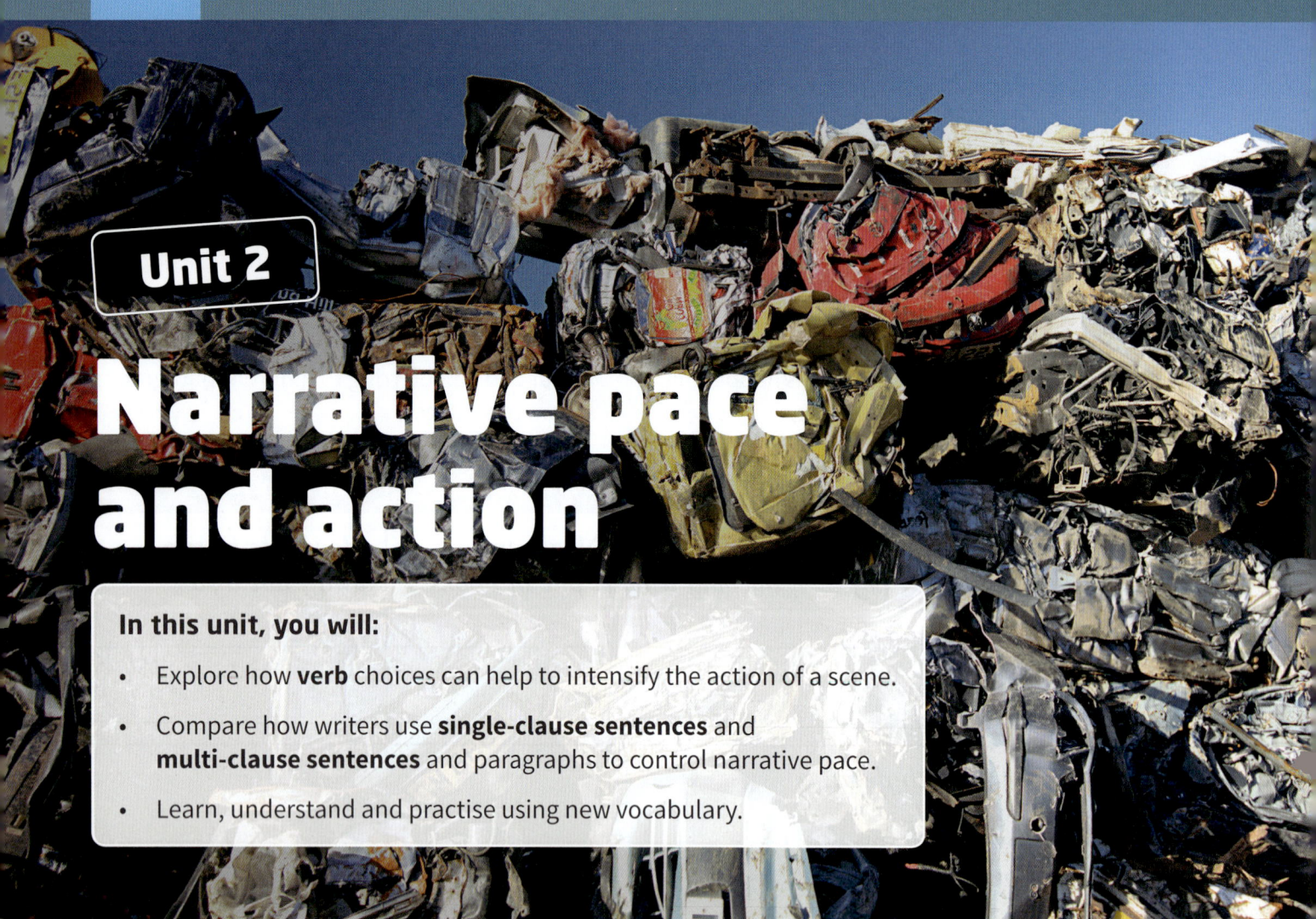

In this unit, you will:

- Explore how **verb** choices can help to intensify the action of a scene.
- Compare how writers use **single-clause sentences** and **multi-clause sentences** and paragraphs to control narrative pace.
- Learn, understand and practise using new vocabulary.

A story starts with the words on the page but comes to life in the reader's imagination. The verbs a writer chooses can influence the way a reader **visualises** the action of a story. When you're writing your own stories you need to consider whether the verbs you choose fit the action you are describing.

The extract on page 13 comes from *Stormbreaker* by Anthony Horowitz, a novel about a teenage spy named Alex Rider. Here, Alex is hiding in his dead uncle's car, a BMW, which is parked in a scrapyard where vehicles are taken to be destroyed.

Key terms

multi-clause sentence a sentence made up of more than one clause, each with its own verb

single-clause sentence (also known as a simple sentence) a sentence with one main clause

verb a word that identifies actions, thoughts, feelings or a state of being

visualise create a picture in your mind

Ready, set, go!

As you read the extract opposite, think about how the writer's language choices help you to picture the scene.

Unit 2: Narrative pace and action

Extract from *Stormbreaker* by Anthony Horowitz
496 words

And then something hit the BMW with such force that Alex cried out, his whole body caught in a massive shock wave that tore him away from the steering wheel and threw him helplessly into the back. The roof buckled and three huge metal fingers tore through the skin of the car like a fork through an eggshell, trailing dust and sunlight. One of the fingers grazed the side of his head … any closer and it would have cracked his skull. Alex yelled as blood trickled over his eye. He tried to move, then was jerked back a second time as the car was yanked off the ground and tilted high up in the air.

He couldn't see. He couldn't move. But his stomach lurched as the car swung in an arc, the metal grinding and the light spinning. The BMW had been picked up by the crane. It was going to be put inside the crusher. With him inside.

He tried to raise himself up, to wave through the windows. But the claw of the crane had already flattened the roof, pinning his left leg, perhaps even breaking it. He could feel nothing. He lifted a hand and managed to pound on the back window, but he couldn't break the glass. Even if the workmen were staring at the BMW, they would never see anything moving inside.

His short flight across the junkyard ended with a bone-shattering crash as the crane deposited the car on the iron shelves of the crusher. Alex tried to fight back his sickness and despair and think of what to do.

Any moment now the operator would send the car tipping into the coffin-shaped **trough**. The machine was a Lefort Shear, a slow-motion **guillotine**. At the press of a button, the two wings would close on the car with a joint pressure of five hundred tons. The car, with Alex inside it, would be crushed beyond recognition. And the broken metal – and flesh – would then be chopped into sections. Nobody would ever know what had happened.

He tried with all his strength to free himself. But the roof was too low. His leg was trapped. Then his whole world tilted and he felt himself falling into darkness. The shelves had lifted. The BMW slid to one side and fell the few yards into the trough. Alex felt the metalwork collapsing all around him. The back window exploded and glass showered around his head, dust and diesel fumes punching into his nose and eyes.

There was hardly any daylight now, but looking out of the back, he could see the huge steel head of the **piston** that would push what was left of the car through the exit hole on the other side.

The engine tone of the Lefort Shear changed as it prepared for the final act. The metal wings shuddered. In a few seconds' time the two of them would meet, crumpling the BMW like a paper bag.

Will Alex escape?

---

trough – a long, narrow, open container
guillotine – a machine with a heavy blade for cutting (a guillotine was originally a machine for beheading criminals, used in the past in France)
piston – a sliding disc or cylinder fitting closely inside a tube in which it moves up and down as part of an engine or pump

1.2 Chapter 1: Plot and pace

⚡ Word power

Re-read the extract on page 13. Pay particular attention to the target words listed below. As you read, think about what each of the words might mean in the extract.

Your target words for this section are:

- buckled
- yanked
- pinning
- deposited
- crumpling

These target words have been highlighted in blue in the extract on page 13. All the target words in this section are verbs.

What would it feel like to be in a car grabbed by a crane?

1 a. Decide what impression the highlighted word gives you of the action of the scene from the options below.

'The roof buckled'

The word 'buckled' gives me the impression that the car roof has...

cracked   collapsed

disappeared   jumped

b. Give the verb 'buckled' an intensity rating from 1 to 5 (with 5 meaning the verb makes the action sound very intense). Explain your choice of rating.

2 a. Decide what impression the highlighted word gives you of the action of the scene from the options below.

'the car was yanked off the ground'

The word 'yanked' gives me the impression that the car was lifted...

carefully   suddenly

slowly   violently

b. Give the verb 'yanked' an intensity rating from 1 to 5, then explain your rating.

Unit 2: Narrative pace and action

3 'But the claw of the crane had already flattened the roof, pinning his left leg'

Here, the word 'pinning' is used as a verb meaning holding firmly. Rewrite this quotation, replacing the word 'pinning' with an alternative verb that gives the same meaning.

4 'the crane deposited the car on the iron shelves of the crusher'

Look up the word 'deposited' in the Target word list on pages 174–175. Rewrite this quotation, replacing the word 'deposited' with an alternative verb that gives the same meaning but makes the action sound more violent.

5 Look again at the final paragraph of the extract, where Horowitz describes what will happen to the car Alex is trapped in. Explain how the choice of the verb 'crumpling' adds to the effectiveness of the **simile** used.

> **Key term**
>
> **simile** a comparison that uses the word 'like' or 'as', e.g. *as cold as ice*

Knowledge and understanding

Look back at the extract on page 13 and answer the following questions.

1 Re-read the opening paragraph of the extract and place the following events into the correct order.
- The car is lifted off the ground.
- Alex cries out.
- Alex is thrown into the back of the car.
- The claw of the crane buckles the roof of the car.

2 List two different ways in which Alex is injured.

3 How does Alex try to let the workmen know he is trapped in the car?

4 The crusher is described as having a 'coffin-shaped trough'. Explain why you think Horowitz has chosen the adjective 'coffin-shaped'.

5 Look again at the sentence:

> 'The car, with Alex inside it, would be crushed beyond recognition.'

Using your own words, explain what the words 'beyond recognition' mean.

6 Create a storyboard with pictures and captions showing the action of the scene. In your storyboard present the key events in the correct order.

15

1.2 Chapter 1: Plot and pace

✏️ Writing skills

When creating action scenes, writers can control the pace of the narrative through their choice of sentences and use of punctuation.

Look again at the following sentence from the extract on page 13. The use of single-clause sentences creates a faster **rhythm**, increasing the narrative pace. The longer, multi-clause sentence adds descriptive detail, slowing the pace a little, before it increases again. The paragraph reaches a climax with the final sentence fragment, when the full horror of Alex's situation is revealed.

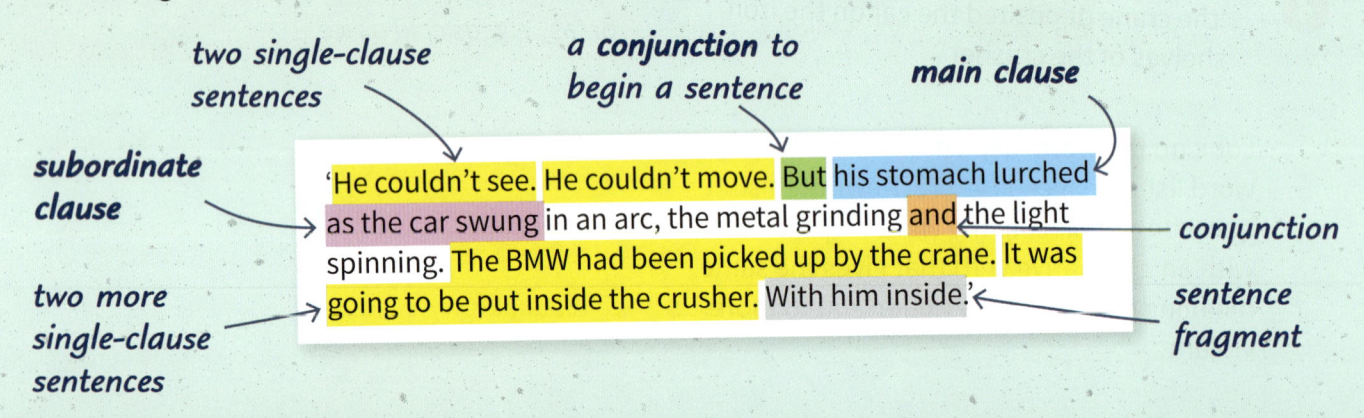

> 'He couldn't see. He couldn't move. But his stomach lurched as the car swung in an arc, the metal grinding and the light spinning. The BMW had been picked up by the crane. It was going to be put inside the crusher. With him inside.'

- two single-clause sentences → "He couldn't see. He couldn't move."
- a conjunction to begin a sentence → "But"
- main clause → "his stomach lurched"
- subordinate clause → "as the car swung"
- conjunction → "and"
- two more single-clause sentences → "The BMW had been picked up by the crane. It was going to be put inside the crusher."
- sentence fragment → "With him inside."

1

a. Rewrite the following multi-clause sentence as a series of shorter single-clause sentences and fragments.

> 'And then something hit the BMW with such force that Alex cried out, his whole body caught in a massive shock wave that tore him away from the steering wheel and threw him helplessly into the back.'

b. What effect do the changes you have made have on the narrative pace? Which version do you think is more powerful?

2 Writers also use punctuation to control the pace of the narrative. An **ellipsis** (…) can be used to add a pause into a sentence to encourage the reader either to think about what they have just read, or to anticipate what comes next. A pair of **dashes** (–) act like brackets to separate out information.

a. Explain what effects are created by the ellipsis and dashes in the following sentences.

> 'One of the fingers grazed the side of his head … any closer and it would have cracked his skull.'

> 'And the broken metal – and flesh – would then be chopped into sections.'

b. Write two of your own sentences – one including an ellipsis and the other including dashes – describing a moment of action. This could be someone scoring a goal or tripping when running to catch a bus, for example.

Unit 2: Narrative pace and action

3 Copy and complete the table below to help you compare how the writer of the extract from *Once* on page 7 and the writer of the extract from *Stormbreaker* control narrative pace in these extracts. Remember to identify the features and comment on the impact these have.

Features used to control narrative pace	*Once*	*Stormbreaker*
Paragraphs	Many very short paragraphs containing single ideas, as if following a child's thought processes as he moves closer. This slows the narrative pace.	
Sentences		
Punctuation		

! Check your skills

Write a dramatic scene of an action-packed moment such as a car crash. Think about:

- the verbs you choose to intensify the action
- how to use different sentence lengths and forms to control the narrative pace
- including dashes and an ellipsis to create deliberate effects
- using paragraphs to make the sequence of events clear.

Check your work for any grammar, spelling and punctuation errors.

Key terms

conjunction a linking word that joins words or groups of words together, e.g. *if, but, and*

dash a punctuation mark (–) used to show a pause

ellipsis a punctuation mark (…) used to show words are missing, to allow a pause or suggest that something is going to happen

main clause a clause that contains a subject and a verb, and makes sense on its own

rhythm the pattern made by the 'beats' in language or music

subordinate clause a clause that adds information to a main clause but that can't work as a sentence on its own

17

1.3 Chapter 1: Plot and pace

Unit 3

A sense of place

In this unit, you will:

- Identify how a writer uses **adverbs** of time and place to help establish **setting**.
- Explore how language and **imagery** contribute to mood and **atmosphere**.
- Learn, understand and practise using new vocabulary.

Writers use a range of techniques to help readers imagine the fictional worlds they create. From idyllic islands to haunted houses, a writer's language choices can change the way readers visualise the settings described and give the reader an impression of the mood and atmosphere of these places. This then provides a suitable background against which the plot of the story can unfold.

The extract on page 19 is the opening of the novel *The Island at the End of Everything* by Kiran Millwood Hargrave. In the opening of a novel, the writer has to establish the setting, helping the reader to understand where and when the story takes place. It can be helpful to think about the setting as the stage upon which the plot of a story takes place. The setting of *The Island at the End of Everything* is the island of Culion, in the Philippines.

Key terms

adverb a word that gives more detail about a verb, an adjective or another adverb

atmosphere the feeling or mood given by the writing, often linked to the setting or situation

imagery writing that creates a picture in the reader's mind or appeals to other senses

setting the time and place where the action of a story happens

Ready, set, go!

As you read the extract opposite, think about the impression you get of the island of Culion.

Unit 3: A sense of place

Extract from *The Island at the End of Everything* by Kiran Millwood Hargrave
509 words

There are some places you would not want to go.

Even if I told you that we have oceans clear and blue as summer skies, filled with sea turtles and dolphins, or forest-covered hills lush with birds that call through air thick with warmth. Even if you knew how beautiful the quiet is here, clean and fresh as a glass bell ringing. But nobody comes here because they want to.

My *nanay* told me this is how they brought her, but says it is always the same, no matter who you are or where you come from.

From your house you travel on horse or by foot, then on a boat. The men who row it cover their noses and mouths with cloths stuffed with herbs so they don't have to share your breath. They will not help you on to the boat although your head aches and two weeks ago your legs began to hurt, then to numb. Maybe you stumble towards them, and they duck. They'd rather you rolled over their backs and into the sea than touch you. You sit and clutch your bundle of things from home, what you saved before it was burned. Clothes, a doll, some books, letters from your mother.

Somehow, it is always dusk when you approach.

The island changes from a dark dot to a green heaven on the horizon. High on a cross-topped cliff that slopes towards the sea is a field of white flowers, looping strangely. It is not until you are closer that you see it forms the shape of an eagle, and it is not until you are very close that you see it is made of stones. This is when your heart hardens in your chest, like petals turning to pebbles. Nanay says the white eagle's meaning is known across all the surrounding islands, even all the places outside our sea. It means: *stay away. Do not come here unless you have no choice.*

The day is dropping to dark as you come into the harbour. When you step from the boat, the stars are setting out their little lights. Someone will be there to welcome you. They understand.

The men who brought you leave straight away, though they are tired. They have not spoken to you in the days or hours you spent with them. The splash of oars fades to the sound of waves lapping the beach. They will burn the boat when they get back, as they did your house.

You look at the person who greeted you. You are changed now. Like flowers into stones, day into night. You will always be heavier, darkened, marked. Touched.

Nanay says that in the places outside, they have many names for our home. The island of the living dead. The island of no return. The island at the end of everything.

You are on Culion, where the oceans are blue and clear as summer skies. Culion, where sea turtles dig the beaches and the trees brim with fruit.

Culion, island of **lepers**. Welcome home.

---

lepers – people who have leprosy, an infectious disease that makes part of the body waste away

Why did the men not want any contact with their passengers?

1.3 Chapter 1: Plot and pace

⚡ Word power

Re-read the extract on page 19. Pay particular attention to the target words listed below. As you read, think about what each of the target words might mean in context.

Your target words for this section are:

- lush
- bundle
- dropping
- marked
- touched

These target words have been highlighted in blue in the extract on page 19.

Which part of the island looks lush?

Unit 3: A sense of place

1 'Lush' is an adjective that means growing thickly and strongly.

  a. In the extract, what part of the island is described as 'lush'? What impression does this adjective help to give you about this place?

  b. Write a sentence describing a place in your local area, using the word 'lush' in a similar way.

2 a. Look again at the following sentence from the extract:

> 'You sit and clutch your bundle of things from home, what you saved before it was burned.'

  Look up the word 'bundle' in the Target word list on pages 174–175. Three definitions are given. Which do you think is the correct definition for the way 'bundle' is used in this sentence?

  b. Use the word 'bundle' as a verb in a sentence describing yourself packing your school bag.

3 'The day is dropping to dark as you come into the harbour.'

Why do you think Millwood Hargrave has used the word 'dropping' in this sentence?

4 Find where the words 'marked' and 'touched' have been used in the extract. Millwood Hargrave uses these words to suggest how the narrator has changed. Do you think this is a positive or negative change? Give reasons for your answer, referring to the use of the words 'marked' and 'touched'.

💡 Knowledge and understanding

Look back at the extract on page 19 and answer the following questions.

1 List three details about the island that suggest it is a pleasant place.

2 The narrator describes the journey to the island. Who does the narrator say told her about this journey?

3 a. Pick out two ways the men who row the boat to the island avoid any form of contact with the passengers.

  b. Explain what impression these details give you about the passengers.

4 a. What does the narrator say can be seen on the cliff as you approach the island?

  b. What does the narrator say the meaning of this is?

5 The novel is set on the island of Culion. List three other names that are given to this place.

21

1.3 Chapter 1: Plot and pace

📖 Reading skills

1 Writers can use adverbs of place to say where something happens, for example:

> He ran **to the end of the street**.
> ↑ adverb of place

Copy and complete the following table to identify more adverbs of place from the extract and explain the information they give about the setting.

Adverb of place	What they tell you about the setting
'The island changes from a dark dot to a green heaven on the horizon.'	The adverb 'on the horizon' suggests how far the island is at first and how it changes as you get closer.

2 Writers use adverbs of time to say when or how often something happens, for example:

> I must be home **by midnight**.
> ↑ adverb of time

> **Sometimes** he will phone if he's going to be late.

adverb of time

Look again at the description of the journey to the island, from the paragraph beginning 'From your house you travel…' to the paragraph ending '*Do not come here unless you have no choice.*' Pick out any adverbs of time you can identify from this section and explain what they tell you about the journey to the island.

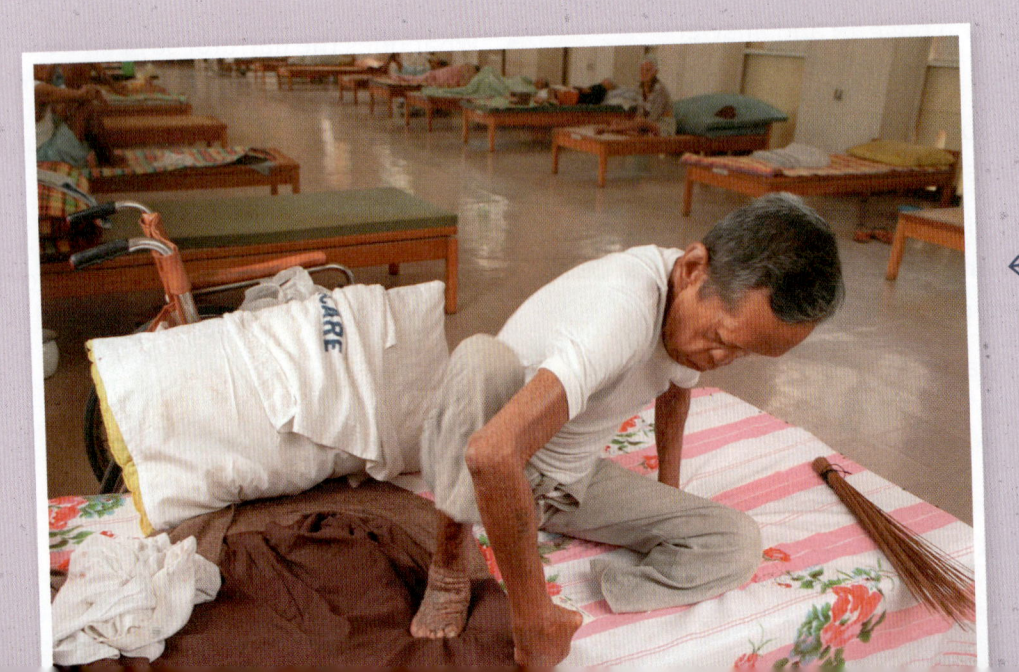

There is still a hospital for lepers on Culion.

22

Unit 3: A sense of place

3 Writers can use imagery to help readers to picture the settings they create.

Copy and complete the following table to identify the different techniques Millwood Hargrave uses and the impression these give of the setting. Remember to add your own example to the last row of the table.

Technique	Example	The impression this gives
Simile	'oceans clear and blue as summer skies'	This simile gives the impression...
Metaphor	'a green heaven'	
	'clean and fresh as a glass bell ringing'	

! Check your skills

Re-read the extract on page 19 from the paragraph beginning 'The day is dropping to dark...' to the end.

How does the writer use imagery to build a picture of the island of Culion in this section of the text? Remember to include in your answer:

- brief quotations of words and phrases from the section that you think are particularly effective in helping to give an impression of Culion
- your own ideas and explanations about the impression these quotations give you
- terms such as 'imagery' to show you understand the specific features the writer has used.

1.4 Chapter 1: Plot and pace

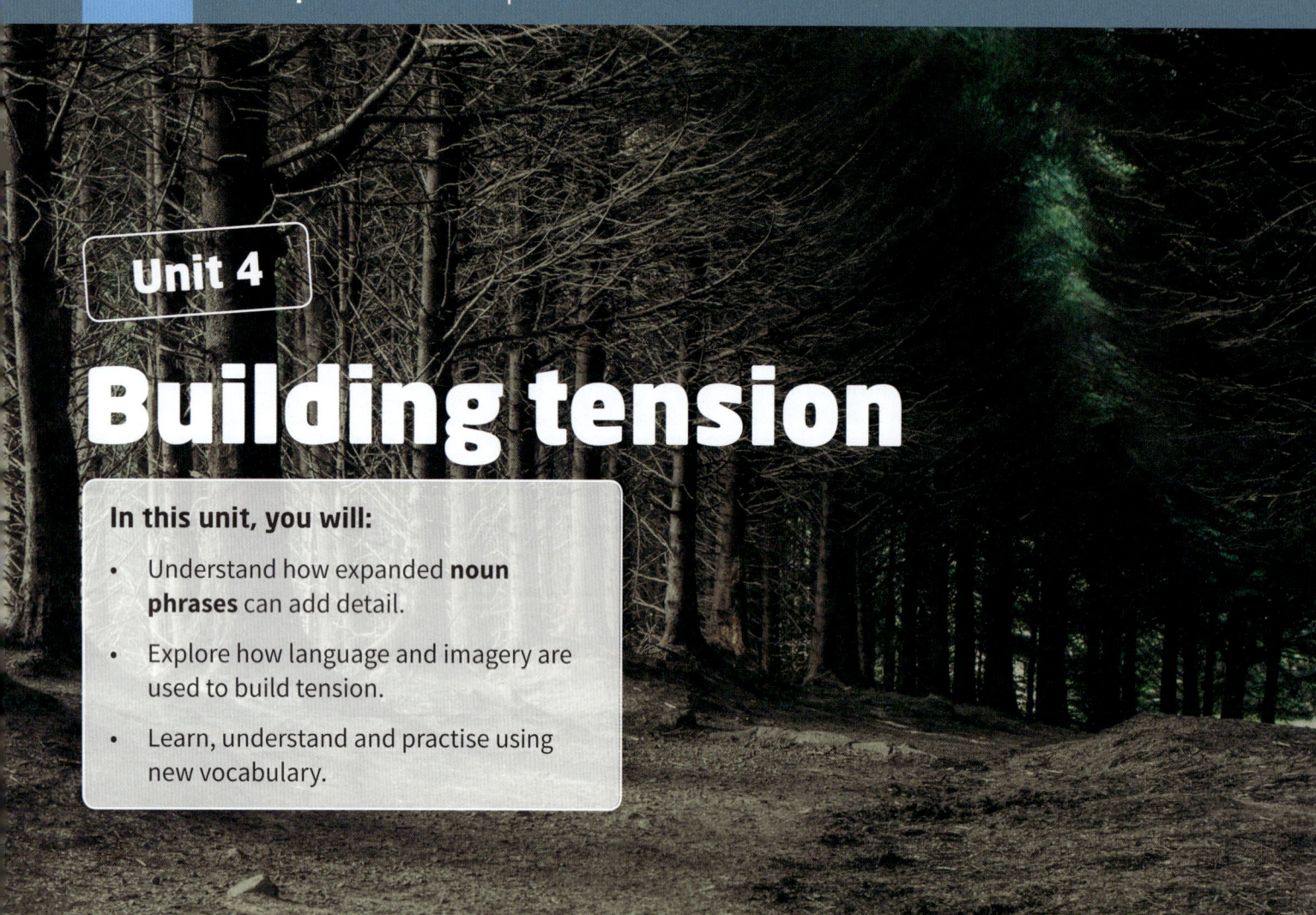

Unit 4

Building tension

In this unit, you will:

- Understand how expanded **noun phrases** can add detail.
- Explore how language and imagery are used to build tension.
- Learn, understand and practise using new vocabulary.

In fiction, writers often want to build tension or **suspense** to keep readers on the edge of their seats. This is often true in horror stories where the language and imagery are deliberately used to create a sense of fear. The extract on page 25 is taken from 'The Legend of Sleepy Hollow', a horror story by the American writer Washington Irving, which was first published in 1820.

In this extract, a schoolteacher called Ichabod Crane is riding his horse, Gunpowder, through the woods of Sleepy Hollow late one night on his way home. According to local legend, these woods are haunted by several ghosts, including a headless horseman. The extract begins as Ichabod rides towards a tree that is supposed to be haunted by the ghost of a murdered British spy named Major André.

Key terms

noun a word used to name a place, person, feeling, thing or idea

noun phrase a group of words that has a **noun** as its head or key word. All the words in the group tell us more about the head noun, e.g. *a big muddy puddle* ('puddle' is the head noun)

suspense an anxious or uncertain feeling while waiting for something to happen or become known

Ready, set, go!

As you read the extract opposite, think about how the writer builds tension in the extract.

Unit 4: Building tension

**Extract adapted from 'The Legend of Sleepy Hollow'
by Washington Irving
375 words**

As Ichabod approached this fearful tree, he began to whistle; he thought his whistle was answered; it was but a blast sweeping sharply through the dry branches. As he approached a little nearer, he thought he saw something white, hanging in the midst of the tree: he paused and ceased whistling but, on looking more narrowly, perceived that it was a place where the tree had been **scathed** by lightning, and the white wood laid bare. Suddenly he heard a groan – his teeth chattered […]: it was but the rubbing of one huge bough upon another, as they were swayed about by the breeze. He passed the tree in safety, but new perils lay before him.

About two hundred yards from the tree, a small **brook** crossed the road, and ran into a marshy and thickly wooded **glen**, known by the name of Wiley's Swamp. A few rough logs, laid side by side, served for a bridge over this stream. On that side of the road where the brook entered the wood, a group of oaks and chestnuts, matted thick with wild grapevines, threw a **cavernous** gloom over it. To pass this bridge was the severest trial. It was at this identical spot that the unfortunate André was captured […]. This has ever since been considered a haunted stream, and fearful are the feelings of the schoolboy who has to pass it alone after dark.

As he approached the stream, his heart began to thump; he summoned up, however, all his resolution, gave his horse **half a score** of kicks in the ribs, and attempted to dash briskly across the bridge; but instead of starting forward, the **perverse** old animal […] ran **broadside** against the fence. Ichabod, whose fears increased with the delay, jerked the reins on the other side, and kicked […] with the contrary foot: it was all in vain; his steed started, it is true, but it was only to plunge to the opposite side of the road into a thicket of brambles and alder bushes. […] In the dark shadow of the **grove**, on the **margin** of the brook, he **beheld** something huge, misshapen and towering. It **stirred** not, but seemed gathered up in the gloom, like some gigantic monster ready to spring upon the traveller.

---

scathed – burned or scorched
brook – stream
glen – a narrow valley
cavernous – huge and often empty or dark
half a score – ten (a score is 20)
perverse – deliberately doing something different from what is reasonable or normal
broadside – sideways on
grove – a small wood or group of trees
margin – an edge or border
beheld – saw
stirred – moved

1.4 Chapter 1: Plot and pace

⚡ Word power

Re-read the extract on page 25. Pay particular attention to the target words listed below. As you read, think about what each of the target words might mean in context.

Your target words for this section are:

- matted
- trial
- resolution
- contrary
- misshapen

These target words have been highlighted in blue in the extract on page 25.

> **Key term**
>
> **prefix** a word or group of letters placed in front of another word to add to or change its meaning

1. If something is 'matted' it is tangled in a mass. What impression does Irving's use of the word 'matted' give you about the woods?

2. Look again at the following sentence from the extract:

   > 'To pass this bridge was the severest trial.'

   Look up the word 'trial' in the Target word list on pages 174–175. Four definitions are given. Which do you think is the correct definition for the way 'trial' is used in this sentence? Give reasons for your answer.

3. If a person has 'resolution' it means they have great determination. Look again at the extract on page 25. How does Ichabod Crane show his resolution?

4. The phrase 'on the contrary' is used when someone is presenting an opposite point of view. Find where the word 'contrary' is used on page 25 and explain what it means in this context.

5. > 'In the dark shadow of the grove, on the margin of the brook, he beheld something huge, misshapen and towering.'

   a. Think about how the **prefix** 'mis-' is used in different words such as:

   misunderstand   misjudge   misuse

   Explain what you think the prefix 'mis-' means.

   b. Explain what the word 'misshapen' suggests about what Ichabod sees here.

26

Unit 4: Building tension

Knowledge and understanding

Look back at the extract on page 25 and answer the following questions.

1
a. In the first paragraph, what do you think Ichabod thinks he sees in the tree?

b. What does Ichabod actually see in the tree?

2
a. In the first paragraph, what sound does Ichabod hear that suddenly scares him?

b. Pick out a brief quotation that shows that Ichabod is scared by this sound.

c. Explain in your own words what has caused this sound.

3 Re-read the second paragraph of the extract on page 25. Use the information from this paragraph to draw a map of the area through which Ichabod is travelling. On your map, mark the following locations:

- the tree
- the bridge
- the road
- the wood
- the stream.

4 How can you tell Ichabod is scared as he approaches the stream?

5 Using evidence from the text, explain what you think Ichabod sees at the end of the extract.

1.4 Chapter 1: Plot and pace

✏️ Writing skills

1 In the extract, Irving uses noun phrases to add descriptive details about the setting. Look at the following examples:

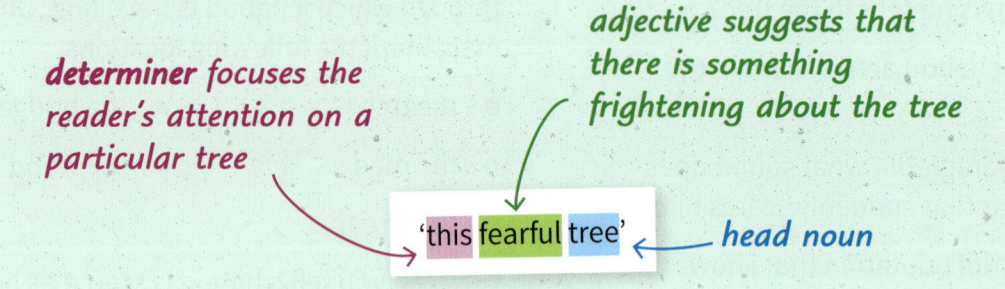

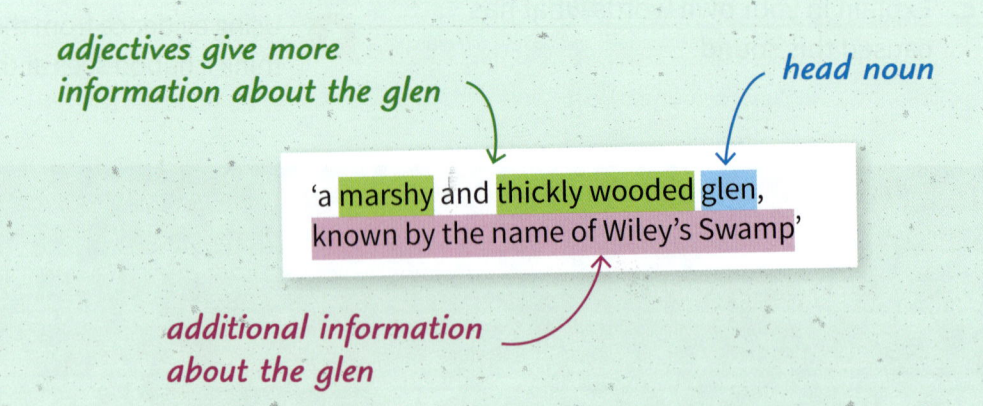

determiner focuses the reader's attention on a particular tree

adjective suggests that there is something frightening about the tree

'this fearful tree' ← *head noun*

adjectives give more information about the glen

head noun

'a marshy and thickly wooded glen, known by the name of Wiley's Swamp'

additional information about the glen

Note that more detail about the head noun can be placed both before and after it. Write your own expanded noun phrases to describe the setting of this story. Copy and complete the following table to help you do this.

Determiner	Adjective(s)	Head noun	Additional information about the head noun
		bridge	
		wood	
		stream	

28

Unit 4: Building tension

2 In the extract, Irving's choice of language and imagery helps to build tension. For example, in the descriptive detail 'cavernous gloom', the choice of the adjective 'cavernous' makes the shadows thrown by the woods sound deep and endless, encouraging the reader to imagine what might be hiding in this gloom.

  a. Pick out two more descriptive details that you think help to create tension.

  b. For each detail you pick out, explore the **connotations** of the vocabulary chosen and explain how this helps to build a sense of fear.

Key terms

connotation an idea or meaning suggested by a word or phrase

determiner a word that comes before a noun and gives more information about it, such as which one it is, how many there are, where it is and whose it is, e.g. *an*, *that* or *some*

protagonist main character

! Check your skills

Write a scene that builds tension and creates a sense of fear. This could be a scene in a story that describes the **protagonist** exploring what appears to be a derelict house and then hearing a strange noise…

In your writing you should think about:

- using expanded noun phrases to add details that help to create a sense of fear
- the connotations of the vocabulary you choose
- how you can use language and imagery to build tension.

When you have completed your first draft, check your work for any grammar, spelling and punctuation errors. Correct these to complete a final draft of your writing.

What, or who, do you think you might find in a house like this?

29

1.5 Chapter 1: Plot and pace

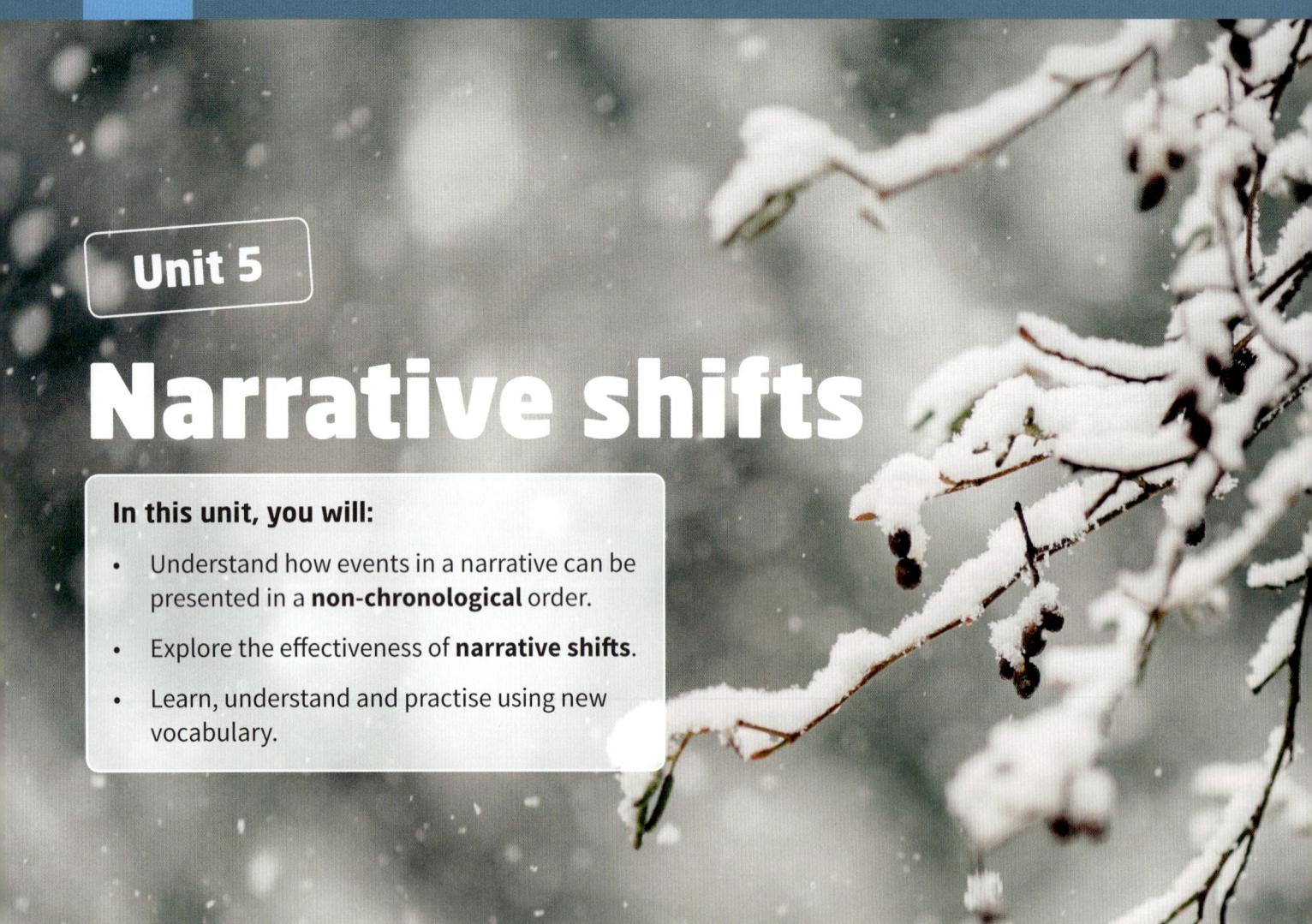

Unit 5

Narrative shifts

In this unit, you will:

- Understand how events in a narrative can be presented in a **non-chronological** order.
- Explore the effectiveness of **narrative shifts**.
- Learn, understand and practise using new vocabulary.

Every story has a beginning, a middle and an end, but the order in which the events of a story are presented to the reader is up to the writer. Some writers might choose to tell a story in **chronological order**, but others might move backwards and forwards in time as the narrative unfolds. This can give the reader different insights into the story.

The extract on page 31 is from the beginning of the novel *The Secret History* by Donna Tartt. In this extract, Richard – who tells the story – reveals that he was involved in the murder of one of his friends, Bunny.

Key terms

chronological order the order in which actions or events happen

narrative shift a change of location, narrator or time in a story

non-chronological not presented in the order in which things occurred

Ready, set, go!

As you read the extract opposite, think about how the narrator moves backwards and forwards in time to reveal details of Bunny's murder and the consequences of this.

Unit 5: Narrative shifts

Extract from *The Secret History* by Donna Tartt
435 words

The snow in the mountains was melting and Bunny had been dead for several weeks before we came to understand the gravity of our situation. He'd been dead for ten days before they found him, you know. It was one of the biggest manhunts in **Vermont** history – state troopers, the FBI, even an army helicopter; the college closed, the **dye** factory in Hampden shut down, people coming from New Hampshire, upstate New York, as far away as Boston.

It is difficult to believe that Henry's modest plan could have worked so well despite these unforeseen events. We hadn't intended to hide the body where it couldn't be found. In fact, we hadn't hidden it at all but had simply left it where it fell in hopes that some luckless passer-by would stumble over it before anyone even noticed he was missing. This was a tale that told itself simply and well: the loose rocks, the body at the bottom of the **ravine** with a clean break in the neck, and the muddy skidmarks of dug-in heels pointing the way down; a hiking accident, no more, no less, and it might have been left at that, at quiet tears and a small funeral, had it not been for the snow that fell that night; it covered him without a trace, and ten days later, when the thaw finally came, the state troopers and the FBI and the searchers from the town all saw that they had been walking back and forth over his body until the snow above it was packed down like ice.

Why didn't the search find the body?

It is difficult to believe that such an uproar took place over an act for which I was partially responsible, even more difficult to believe I could have walked through it – the cameras, the uniforms, the black crowds sprinkled over Mount Cataract like ants in a sugar bowl – without incurring a blink of suspicion. But walking through it all was one thing; walking away, unfortunately, has proved to be quite another, and though once I thought I had left that ravine forever on an April afternoon long ago, now I am not so sure. Now the searchers have departed, and life has grown quiet around me, I have come to realise that while for years I might have imagined myself to be somewhere else, in reality I have been there all the time: up at the top by the muddy **wheel-ruts** in the new grass, where the sky is dark over the shivering apple blossoms and the first chill of the snow that will fall that night is already in the air.

Vermont – a state in the north-east of the USA
dye – a substance used for changing the colour of something
ravine – a deep narrow gorge with steep sides
wheel-ruts – grooves in the ground made by wheels

1.5 Chapter 1: Plot and pace

⚡ Word power

Re-read the extract on page 31. Pay particular attention to the target words listed below. As you read, think about what each of the words might mean in this context.

Your target words for this section are:

- gravity
- modest
- luckless
- uproar
- act
- incurring

These target words have been highlighted in blue in the extract on page 31.

What did the friends do and what are the consequences?

1. Gravity is the force that pulls everything towards the centre of Earth or towards another physical body. However, gravity can also mean the importance or seriousness of a situation and is linked to the adjective 'grave', which means serious. Look again at the following sentence:

> 'The snow in the mountains was melting and Bunny had been dead for several weeks before we came to understand the gravity of our situation.'

Rewrite the sentence, replacing the word 'gravity' with 'importance' or 'seriousness'. Explain which word you think fits the meaning of the sentence best.

2. Look up the word 'modest' in the Target word list on pages 174–175. Four definitions are given. Which do you think is the correct definition for the way 'modest' is used in this sentence? Give reasons for your answer.

3. If someone is luckless, they are unlucky. Create your own definitions for the following words that use the **suffix** '-less'.

a. fearless
b. helpless
c. hopeless
d. tasteless

Key term

suffix a group of letters joined to the end of a word to make another word, e.g. forget*ful*, kind*ness*, entertain*er*

32

Unit 5: Narrative shifts

4 'It is difficult to believe that such an uproar took place over an act for which I was partially responsible'

In this context, 'act' means something someone has done and 'uproar' means an outburst of noise or excitement or anger.

a. What is the action that has caused the uproar?

b. Write your own sentence using the word 'act' or 'uproar' to describe someone doing something that causes great excitement, such as a footballer scoring a winning goal.

5 To 'incur' something difficult or unwelcome is to do or say something that makes it happen, for example:

> *Because I parked in the wrong place I incurred a fine.*

a. Find where the word 'incurring' is used in the extract on page 31. What does the narrator say he didn't incur?

b. Write your own sentence using the word 'incurring' to describe the narrator being punished for Bunny's murder.

Knowledge and understanding

Look back at the extract on page 31 and answer the following questions.

1 What month was Bunny murdered in?

2 How long did it take for Bunny's body to be discovered?

3 What stopped Bunny's body being discovered any sooner?

4 What had the narrator hoped Bunny's death looked like?

5 Pick out one detail from the first paragraph and one detail from the final paragraph that give an impression of the uproar Bunny's death caused. Write a paragraph explaining why you selected these two details.

6 Look again at the sentence from the end of the extract that begins:

> 'Now the searchers have departed…'

Explain what this sentence suggests about the effect Bunny's murder has had on the narrator.

33

1.5 Chapter 1: Plot and pace

Reading skills

1. Create a timeline presenting information about Bunny's murder and its consequences. Include the following events:
   - when Bunny was murdered
   - when the snow fell
   - when Bunny's body was discovered
   - when his murderers realised the seriousness of the situation
   - the point in time the narrator is telling the story from.

2. **a.** Look again at the opening paragraph of the story.

   first sentence → The snow in the mountains was melting and Bunny had been dead for several weeks before we came to understand the gravity of our situation. He'd been dead for ten days before they found him, you know. It was one of the biggest manhunts in Vermont history – state troopers, the FBI, even an army helicopter; the college closed, the dye factory in Hampden shut down, people coming from New Hampshire, upstate New York, as far away as Boston. ← *second sentence*

   The event described in the second sentence (the discovery of Bunny's body) comes before the event described in the first sentence (the murderers' realising their situation is serious). Why do you think the writer makes this shift in time here?

   b. Now look at the final sentence of the opening paragraph. Does the focus of this move backwards or forwards in time? What effect does this create?

   > **Tip** ✓
   >
   > Think about how this sentence links back to the first sentence. You might find it helpful to look back at the timeline you created in Activity 1.

3. Now look at the second and third paragraphs. For each paragraph, identify where the events described come in the chronology of the story. Refer back to the timeline you created to help you to do this.

Unit 5: Narrative shifts

4 Predict how you think the story could continue from this point. You should consider some of the following ideas but could also make your own suggestions. Give reasons for your prediction.

- Focus on the events leading up to Bunny's death.
- Focus on the day Bunny was murdered.
- Focus on the search for Bunny's killers.

'It was one of the biggest manhunts in Vermont history...'

! Check your skills

A typical detective story starts with the discovery of a dead body and then the plot is about finding out who murdered that person. The extract on page 31 is different because it tells you who the murderers are at the beginning.

How effective do you think this extract is as the opening to a novel? In your answer you should comment on:

- the information you learn about Bunny's murder and its consequences
- how the events are presented in a non-chronological order and the effects this creates
- why you think or don't think this is an effective opening to a novel.

35

1.6 Chapter 1: Plot and pace

Unit 6

Reading assessment

The following extract comes from the novel *Life After Life* by Kate Atkinson. In this extract, eight-year-old Ursula is living in a house with her mother Sylvie, her older sister Pamela and her younger brother Teddy, along with their servants, Bridget the housemaid and Mrs Glover the cook. Here, Ursula has had a premonition – a feeling that something bad is going to happen if Bridget leaves the house – and so decides to act in a dangerous way to stop her from leaving.

Read the extract and then answer the questions that follow it. Remember to use the skills you have developed through the chapter to help you to answer these questions.

Extract from *Life After Life* by Kate Atkinson
383 words

Staircases were very dangerous places, according to Sylvie. People died on them. Sylvie always told them not to play at the top of the stairs.

Ursula crept along the carpet runner. Took a quiet breath and then, both hands out in front of her, as if trying to stop a train, she threw herself at the small of Bridget's back. Bridget whipped her head round, mouth and eyes wide in horror at the sight of Ursula. Bridget went flying, toppling down the stairs in a great flurry of arms and legs. Ursula only just managed to stop herself from following in her **wake**. [100 words]

Practice makes perfect.

'The arm's broken, I'm afraid,' Dr Fellowes said. 'You took quite a tumble down those stairs.'

'She's always been a clumsy girl,' Mrs Glover said.

'*Someone* pushed me,' Bridget said. A great bruise bloomed on her forehead, she was holding her hat, the violets crushed.

'Someone?' Sylvie echoed. 'Who? Who would push you downstairs, Bridget?' She looked around the faces in the kitchen. 'Teddy?' Teddy put his hand over his mouth as if he was trying to stop words escaping. Sylvie turned to Pamela. 'Pamela?'

'Me?' Pamela said, **piously** holding both of her outraged hands over her heart like a **martyr**. Sylvie looked at Bridget, who made a little **inclination** of her head towards Ursula. [200 words]

'Ursula?' Sylvie frowned. Ursula stared blankly ahead, a **conscientious objector** about to be shot. 'Ursula,' Sylvie said severely, 'do you know something about this?'

Ursula had done a wicked thing, she had pushed Bridget down the stairs. Bridget might have died and she would have been a murderer now. All she knew was that she *had* to do it. The great sense of dread had come over her and she had to do it.

Unit 6: Reading assessment

300 words

She ran out of the room and hid in one of Teddy's secret hiding places, the cupboard beneath the stairs. After a while the door opened and Teddy crept in and sat on the floor next to her. 'I don't think you pushed Bridget,' he said and slipped his small, warm hand into hers.

'Thank you. I did though.'

'Well, I still love you.'

She might never have come out of that cupboard but the front door clanged and there was a sudden great **commotion** in the hallway.

---

wake – the track left behind something or someone, e.g. the wake left on the water by a moving ship
piously – very religiously
martyr – a person who is made to suffer because of their beliefs, especially religious beliefs
inclination – a slope or slant
conscientious objector – a person who refuses to serve in the armed forces because he or she believes it is morally wrong
commotion – a noisy disturbance or excitement

---

1 Look again at the paragraph beginning 'Ursula crept along the carpet runner'. Pick out three verbs that you think help to intensify the action of this scene. Give reasons for your choices.

2 Re-read the opening three paragraphs of the extract. How does Atkinson build tension in this section? In your answer you should comment on:

- how Atkinson uses language and imagery to build tension
- how sentence lengths and paragraphs are used to control the narrative pace.

3
a. Identify the sentence where the narrative shifts forward after a break in time after Ursula has pushed Bridget down the stairs.

b. Re-read the rest of the extract that follows this sentence. At first the action shifts to the kitchen, but which other location does the narrative move to?

c. Explain why you think Atkinson has chosen to make these narrative shifts.

4 What impression do you get of Ursula from the extract? Refer to the text to support the points you make.

37

2 Genres and themes

Unit 1

Fantasy

In this unit, you will:

- Explore how a writer selects specific details to both create characters and suggest **themes**.
- Create your own character and suggest a theme using Terry Pratchett's work as a model.
- Learn, understand and practise using new vocabulary.

You may be a reader who enjoys a particular **genre** of fiction. You might love to follow the twists and turns of a crime novel or you might be excited by the thought of seeing the future through the eyes of a science-fiction writer. In this chapter, you will encounter extracts from both of these genres, and many more.

From Harry Potter to *A Wizard of Earthsea*, the idea of a young character learning to control their magical powers is a typical theme in fantasy stories. Terry Pratchett, one of the most popular writers of fantasy, had a limitless imagination and a wonderful sense of humour. In this extract, he introduces us to Tiffany, a young magician who is learning to control her power.

Key terms

genre a particular kind of fiction, e.g. history, science fiction, fantasy, horror, romance, thriller, detective

theme an idea or topic that is found in a work of fiction, such as love, power or revenge

Ready, set, go!

As you read the extract opposite, think about how the writer selects specific details to help us learn about this new character and her powers.

Extract from *A Hat Full of Sky* by Terry Pratchett
476 words

She put the mirror down on the rickety table by the bed, stood in the middle of the threadbare rug, shut her eyes, and said:

'See me.' […]

Tiffany opened her eyes. There she was, a few feet away from herself. She could see the back of her own head.

Carefully, she moved around the room, not looking down at the 'her' that was moving, because she found that if she did that then the trick was over.

It was quite difficult, moving like that, but at last she was in front of herself and looking herself up and down.

Brown hair to match brown eyes … there was nothing she could do about that. At least her hair was clean and she'd washed her face.

She had a new dress on, which improved things a bit. It was so unusual to buy new clothes in the Aching family that, of course, it was bought big so that she'd 'grow into it'. But at least it was pale green, and it didn't actually touch the floor. With the shiny new boots and the straw hat she looked … like a farmer's daughter, quite respectable, going off to her first job. It'd have to do.

From here she could see the pointy hat on her head, but she had to look hard for it. It was like a glint in the air, gone as soon as you saw it. That's why she'd been worried about the new straw hat, but it had simply gone through it as if the new hat wasn't there.

This was because, in a way, it wasn't. It was invisible, except in the rain. Sun and wind went straight through, but rain and snow somehow saw it, and treated it as if it were real.

She'd been given it by the greatest witch in the world, a real witch with a black dress and a black hat and eyes that could go through you **like turpentine goes through a sick sheep**. It had been a kind of reward. Tiffany had done magic, serious magic. Before she had done it she hadn't known that she could; when she had been doing it she hadn't known that she was; and after she had done it she hadn't known how she had. Now she had to *learn* how.

'See me not,' she said. The vision of her … or whatever it was, because she was not exactly sure about this trick … vanished.

It had been a shock, the first time she'd done this. But she'd *always* found it easy to see herself, at least in her head. All her memories were like little pictures of herself doing things or watching things, rather than the view from the two holes in the front of her head. There was a part of her that was always watching her.

---

like turpentine goes through a sick sheep – turpentine is used to treat some stomach diseases in sheep. It passes through them very quickly

2.1 Chapter 2: Genres and themes

⚡ Word power

Re-read the extract on page 39. Pay particular attention to the target words listed below. As you read, think about what each of the words might mean in the extract.

Your target words for this section are:

- rickety
- threadbare
- respectable
- glint
- vision

These target words have been highlighted in blue in the extract on page 39.

1 'Rickety' means unstable and likely to collapse and 'threadbare' means thin and tattered with age. Look at the picture above and write a description of it using both these target words.

2 Find the word 'respectable' in the seventh paragraph. Which of the following words is closest in meaning to it?

- shabby
- proper
- concerned

3 A glint is a small flash of light. Look at how it is used in the extract. Write a sentence about the picture opposite, using the word 'glint' as either a **noun** or a **verb**.

4 Look up the word 'vision' in the Target word list on pages 174–175. Two definitions are given. Which do you think is the correct definition for the way 'vision' is used in the extract? Explain the reasons for your choice.

Key terms

noun a word used to name a place, person, feeling, thing or idea, e.g. *the glint*

verb a word that identifies actions, thoughts, feelings or a state of being, e.g. *glinting, glints, glinted*

40

Unit 1: Fantasy

How does the word 'glint' relate to this picture?

Knowledge and understanding

Look back at the extract on page 39 and answer the following questions.

1. In the first sentence, find two words that tell us that Tiffany's family is quite poor. Explain your choices.

2. Re-read the sentence beginning 'Tiffany opened her eyes …' What magical trick has Tiffany succeeded in performing?

3. In the fourth paragraph, what must she prevent herself from doing and why?

4. In the eighth and ninth paragraphs she describes the pointy hat she is wearing. What is unusual about it?

5. Re-read the tenth paragraph. Pratchett tells us about a witch that was important in Tiffany's life. Why do you think she was important?

6. Re-read the final paragraph. Tiffany explains how she sees her memories in her head. How does she see them?

2.1 Chapter 2: Genres and themes

✏️ Writing skills

1 Look at how the writer introduces Tiffany. He tells us about three aspects of her life:
- her family life and **setting**
- her magical powers
- her character.

He weaves all three into this extract.

Re-read the extract and use information from it to complete a table like this (one entry has been done for you):

> **Key term**
>
> **setting** the time and place where the action of a story happens

> **Tip**
>
> You may find that when you start looking for clues to Tiffany's character, you have to read much more carefully. For instance, what can you learn about Tiffany from the last sentence?

Her family life and situation	Her magical powers	Her character
Her family is poor.		

2 In fantasy stories, magical powers usually obey a set of rules. Tiffany's witch's hat represents her magical power and there are rules that govern it.

   a. Which two of the following statements about the hat are true?
- Everyone can see it all the time.
- No one can ever see it except her.
- The hat was a gift from a powerful witch who is teaching her magic.
- It might give away the fact that she's a witch.

   b. Imagine a character of your own with magical powers (for example, invisibility or the ability to fly). What object might your character possess to represent their power and what rules might govern it?

Unit 1: Fantasy

3 Power in the form of magic is a typical theme found in fantasy stories and many stories tell us that magic can be a difficult power to control. Pratchett introduces Tiffany while she is practising one of her magical powers and this enables him to show us that she is still learning to be a witch. Look at the three paragraphs on the right and how they convey information.

Use information from these paragraphs to write your own description of Tiffany trying out her magical power for the first time. Remember that she will never have experienced her magic power before and she doesn't know the rules, so be sure to show that in your writing. You could start with:

Tiffany opened her eyes…

tells us what Tiffany can do

'Tiffany opened her eyes. There she was, a few feet away from herself. She could see the back of her own head.

Carefully, she moved around the room, not looking down at the 'her' that was moving, because she found that if she did that, then the trick was over.

It was quite difficult, moving like that, but at last she was in front of herself and looking herself up and down.'

shows that Tiffany is not yet fully in control of her power and we learn one of the rules

helps us to understand her magical ability and that she still finds it difficult

! Check your skills

What kind of object will represent your character's magical power?

Now it's time for you to present your own magical character.

- Use a table similar to the one in Activity 1 to plan your magical character.

- Write an account of your character trying out their magical power for the first time. Include information about their magical power, character, family life and situation. Choose an item of clothing or an object to represent the magical power and use it to explain more about your character's unusual life.

- Check your writing carefully for any grammar, spelling or punctuation errors.

43

2.2 Chapter 2: Genres and themes

Unit 2

Set in the past

In this unit, you will:

- Understand how a writer's choice of language can help to evoke a historical period.
- Explore how a writer chooses effective language to describe action and setting.
- Learn, understand and practise using new vocabulary.

When we read historical fiction, we are able to travel in our imaginations to previous centuries, so unlike our own time.

The extract on page 45 comes from Leon Garfield's novel *Smith*, which is set in 18th-century London. The hero, Smith, is a 12-year-old pickpocket, living on the streets. One morning he spies a likely victim.

Key term

slang informal words and phrases usually found in speech rather than writing

Ready, set, go!

As you read the extract opposite, think about how Garfield creates a picture of 18th-century London in your mind. What do you see? What might you smell? What might you hear?

Unit 2: Set in the past

Extract from *Smith* by Leon Garfield
461 words

At about half past ten of a cold December morning an old gentleman got furiously out of his carriage, in which he'd been trapped for an hour, shook his red fist at his helpless coachman and the roaring but motionless world, and began to stump up Ludgate Hill.

'**Pick**-pocket! *Pick*-pocket!' shrieked the cathedral birds in a fury.

A country gentleman – judging by his complexion, his clean old-fashioned coat and his broad-legged, lumbering walk which bumped out his pockets in a manner most provoking.

Smith twitched his nose and nipped neatly along like a shadow…

The old man's pace was variable: sometimes it was brisk for his years, then he'd slow down, hesitate, look about him – as if the Town had changed much since last he'd visited and he was now no longer confident of his way. He took one turning, then another; stopped, scratched the crisp edge of his wig, then eyed the **sallow**, seedy city gentry as if to ask the way, till he spied another turn, nodded, briskly took it – and came straight back into Ludgate Hill…

A dingy fellow creaked out of a doorway, like he was hinged on it, and made to accost the old man: but he did not. He'd glimpsed Smith. Looks had been exchanged, shoulders shrugged – and the old villain gave way to the young one.

On went the old gentleman, confident now in his bearings, deeper and deeper into the musty, tottering forest of the Town where Smith hunted fastest and best.

Now a sharpish wind sprang up, and the cathedral birds eyed the **leaden** sky (which looked too thick and heavy to **admit** them), screeched, and flew to the lower **eminence** of **Old Bailey**. Here, they set up a terrific commotion with their legal **brethren**, till both Church and Law **became absorbed** in watching the progress of Smith.

'*Pick*-pocket! *Pick*-pocket! **Jug**-jug-jug him!'

The old gentleman was very deep in Smith's country now, and paused many a time to peer down the shambling lanes and alleys. Then he'd shake his head vaguely and touch at his coat pocket – as if a queer, deep sense had warned him of a pair of sharp eyes fairly cutting into the cloth like scissors. At last he saw something familiar – some landmark he'd remembered – Godliman Street. Yes: he was in Godliman Street…

As suddenly as it had sprung up, the wind died – and the cathedral birds flew back to their dome.

'*Pick*-pocket! *Pick*-pocket!'

The old gentleman began to stump very **particularly** down Godliman Street, eyeing the old, crumbly houses that were lived in by God knew how many quiet, mysterious souls. And, as he went, he seemed to have two shadows – his own and another, a thin cautious shadow that was not so much seen as sensed…

---

pick-pocket – a thief who steals from people's pockets or bags
sallow – unhealthily pale
leaden – of the colour lead; dull grey
admit – let in
eminence – high point

Old Bailey – the Central Criminal Court of England and Wales, commonly referred to as the Old Bailey, where many serious crimes are tried
brethren – an old word for brothers
became absorbed – watched with concentration
jug – a **slang** term for jail
particularly – in a very careful way

2.2 Chapter 2: Genres and themes

⚡ Word power

Re-read the extract on page 45. Pay particular attention to the target words listed below. As you read, think about what each of the words might mean in the extract.

Your target words for this section are:

- provoking
- seedy
- accost
- bearings
- vaguely

These target words have been highlighted in blue in the extract on page 45.

1. Look up 'provoking' in the Target word list on pages 174–175. Why do you think that Smith found the gentleman's bulging pockets so provoking?

2. 'Seedy' means unpleasant, shabby or falling apart. Look at where it is used in the extract. What impression do you get of the people who live in this part of London?

3. When they are investigating a story, reporters sometimes 'accost' important people in the street and ask them questions. Which two words would best describe this activity?

4. When you get your bearings, you become aware of your position relative to your surroundings. Complete the sentence below including the word 'bearings'.

When the bus dropped us off, we struggled...

rude
polite
sudden
gentle
challenging

Explain your choices.

Tip

Look up 'accost' in the Target word list on pages 174–175 if you are unsure.

Unit 2: Set in the past

5. Look up 'vaguely' in the Target word list on pages 174–175. It has two definitions. Which is the correct definition for the way it is used in the extract?

6. Use the image opposite to write a short description of exploring an unfamiliar town or city. Include three of the target words.

How would you describe this place?

Knowledge and understanding

Look back at the extract on page 45 and answer the following questions.

1. In the first paragraph, why is the old gentleman furious?

2. In the fourth paragraph, find a word that tells you that Smith moved quickly.

3. Re-read the fifth paragraph. Which of the following statements is true:
   - The gentleman walked directly to his destination.
   - He stopped and started, walking at different speeds.

4. In the sixth paragraph, how do we learn that London pickpockets recognised each other?

5. In the seventh paragraph, what does the verb 'hunted' tell us about Smith and the old gentleman?

6. Re-read the eighth and ninth paragraphs. Which of the following statements is false?
   - The cathedral birds are fighting the Old Bailey birds.
   - The birds seem to be warning the old gentleman that he is about to have his pockets picked.
   - Both sets of birds are watching Smith.

7. In the final paragraph, what evidence is there that Smith is still following the old gentleman?

47

2.2 Chapter 2: Genres and themes

📖 Reading skills

1 Writers of historical fiction often write in a style of language that echoes the historical setting. Garfield's language and sentence structures are quite old-fashioned. Look at the following paragraph and the notes around it.

old-fashioned term for a man → **fellow**

rarely used verb meaning 'to speak to him in the street' → **accost**

old-fashioned verb meaning 'tried to' or 'looked as if he was going to' → **made to**

passive voice makes the language sound more impersonal and old-fashioned → **Looks had been exchanged, shoulders shrugged**

'A dingy fellow creaked out of a doorway, like he was hinged on it, and made to accost the old man: but he did not. He'd glimpsed Smith. Looks had been exchanged, shoulders shrugged – and the old villain gave way to the young one.'

old-fashioned word for criminal → **villain**

old term for when one person allows another one to take over → **gave way**

Find two more examples of old-fashioned words or **phrases** elsewhere in the passage.

2 a. Garfield chooses words and phrases that conjure up vivid images for the reader. Look again at the following extract and notes on his word choices.

This is normally used to describe a bleak, dark place. → **dingy**

This usually describes a sound but here also conveys an idea about a way of moving. → **creaked**

'A dingy fellow creaked out of a doorway, like he was hinged on it'

This image links with 'creaked' and 'doorway' to show him moving like a rusty hinge opening a door. → **like he was hinged on it**

Replay the scene in your head until you think you are seeing it as Garfield intended it.
- What does the man look like?
- How does he move?
- Why do you think he moved like this?

48

b. In the sentence below, Garfield uses a **metaphor** describing the town as a forest. Write a paragraph explaining the effect this has on the reader, paying special attention to the highlighted words and phrases.

> 'On went the old gentleman, ==confident now in his bearings, deeper and deeper== into the ==musty, tottering== forest of the Town where Smith ==hunted fastest== and ==best==.'

Tip

If you're not sure of the meanings of any of the words, check them in a dictionary.

Key terms

atmosphere the feeling or mood given by the writing, often linked to the setting or situation

metaphor describing something as something else, not meant to be taken literally, e.g. *You are a star*

passive voice when the subject of the sentence is acted on by the verb, e.g. *The window had been broken by the burglar*

phrase a group of words that forms a unit

Ludgate Hill and Fleet Street in Victorian London

! Check your skills

Re-read the following extract from the text.

Write a paragraph about the way that Garfield uses language to create a threatening, violent **atmosphere** in a historical setting. Comment on:

- word choices
- powerful images.

Support your ideas with quotations from the text.

> 'The old gentleman was very deep in Smith's country now, and paused many a time to peer down the shambling lanes and alleys. Then he'd shake his head vaguely and touch at his coat pocket – as if a queer, deep sense had warned him of a pair of sharp eyes fairly cutting into the cloth like scissors.'

49

2.3 Chapter 2: Genres and themes

Unit 3

Invasion!

In this unit, you will:

- Explore how description can help readers to **visualise** the unfamiliar.
- Analyse how verbs and **noun phrases** can create action and excitement.
- Learn, understand and practise using new vocabulary.

Since its invention in the late 19th century, science fiction has been a popular genre. Readers are fascinated by countless tales of alien civilisations, space exploration and the world of the future.

One of the pioneers of the genre was H. G. Wells, whose novel *The War of the Worlds* tells the story of a Martian invasion of England. This was the first time that aliens had been described in English literature and it has had an enormous influence on books and films ever since. In this extract, the **narrator** is driving home in a horse-drawn cart when he sees a terrifying sight.

Key terms

narrator the person who tells the story

noun phrase a group of words that has a noun as its head or key word. All the words in the group tell us more about the head noun, e.g. *a big muddy puddle* ('puddle' is the head noun)

visualise create a picture in your mind

Ready, set, go!

As you read the extract opposite, think about how Wells helps us to imagine the gigantic alien machines.

Unit 3: Invasion!

Extract from *The War of the Worlds* by H. G. Wells
389 words

And this Thing I saw! How can I describe it? A monstrous **tripod**, higher than many houses, striding over the young pine trees, and smashing them aside in its **career**; a walking engine of glittering metal, striding now across the heather; **articulate** ropes of steel dangling from it, and the clattering tumult of its passage mingling with the riot of the thunder. A flash, and it came out vividly, **heeling** over one way with two feet in the air, to vanish and reappear almost instantly as it seemed, with the next flash, a hundred yards nearer. Can you imagine a **milking stool** tilted and bowled violently along the ground? That was the impression those instant flashes gave. But instead of a milking stool imagine it a great body of machinery on a tripod stand.

Then suddenly the trees in the pine wood ahead of me were parted, as brittle reeds are parted by a man thrusting through them; they were snapped off and driven headlong, and a second huge tripod appeared, rushing, as it seemed, headlong towards me. And I was galloping hard to meet it! At the sight of the second monster my nerve went altogether. Not stopping to look again, I **wrenched** the horse's head hard round to the right and in another moment the **dog cart** had heeled over upon the horse; the **shafts** smashed noisily, and I was flung sideways and fell heavily into a shallow pool of water.

I crawled out almost immediately, and crouched, my feet still in the water, under a clump of **furze**. The horse lay motionless (his neck was broken, poor brute!) and by the lightning flashes I saw the black bulk of the overturned dog cart and the silhouette of the wheel still spinning slowly. In another moment the colossal mechanism went striding by me, and passed uphill towards Pyrford.

Seen nearer, the Thing was incredibly strange […]. Machine it was, with a ringing metallic pace, and long, flexible, glittering tentacles (one of which gripped a young pine tree) swinging and rattling about its strange body. […] Behind the main body was a huge mass of white metal like a gigantic fisherman's basket, and puffs of green smoke squirted out from the joints of the limbs as the monster swept by me. And in an instant it was gone.

Does this milking stool help you to visualise the 'Thing'?

---

tripod – a three-legged stand (like those used to support cameras)
career – an old use of the word to mean a fast journey
articulate – having joints or jointed segments (like an articulated lorry)
heeling – turning

milking stool – a low three-legged stool used by someone milking a cow
wrenched – pulled sharply
dog cart – a light horse-drawn vehicle
shafts – long poles that connect a horse to a cart
furze – a sort of shrub

2.3 Chapter 2: Genres and themes

⚡ **Word power**

Re-read the extract on page 51. Pay particular attention to the target words listed below. As you read, think about what each of the words might mean in the extract.

Your target words for this section are:

- tumult
- mingling
- headlong
- bulk

These target words have been highlighted in blue in the extract on page 51.

> **Key term**
>
> **synonym** a word that means the same or almost the same as another word, e.g. 'glad' is a synonym for 'happy'

1 A tumult is a loud, confused noise but it can also mean chaos and disorder. Look at where it is used in the first paragraph. Choose one word to complete each sentence below.

  a. When the monster appeared above us, a tumult of .... broke out.

   shouting   running   silence

  b. The village was in a state of .... and tumult.

   calm   fear   desertion

2 Look up the word 'mingling' in the Target word list on pages 174–175. Which of the following is the closest **synonym**?

   stamping   mixing   clashing   smashing

3 The word 'headlong' is used twice in the second paragraph to denote speed and direction. Which two of these actions could be done headlong?

   wander   dash   rush   crawl

Unit 3: Invasion!

4 Look at the two meanings of 'bulk' in the Target word list on pages 174–175. Which is the correct meaning for how the word is used in the extract? Be prepared to explain your choice.

5 Describe a scene in which a police officer chases a suspect through a crowded marketplace. Include at least three of the target words.

What would happen if a police officer chased a suspect through this scene?

Knowledge and understanding

Look back at the extract on page 51 and answer the following questions.

1 Re-read the first paragraph. Which two of the statements below are true?

- There was a thunderstorm.
- The tripod moved very slowly.
- The tripod flew above the houses.
- The tripod damaged the trees.

2 In the second paragraph, the narrator says that he 'wrenched the horse's head hard round to the right'. Why did he do this?

3 In the third paragraph, why do you think the narrator crouched under a shrub?

4 Use the information in the extract to draw a sketch of the tripod. Label each part using words from the text.

53

2.3 Chapter 2: Genres and themes

✏️ Writing skills

1 This is an action-packed episode and Wells wants the reader to be able to visualise the tripods clearly. He does this through choosing his verbs carefully and using noun phrases to help us imagine the scene.

Re-read the extract below. The verbs (highlighted orange) and some noun phrases (highlighted green) in this long sentence have been annotated so that you can see how they help to create a strong picture in our minds.

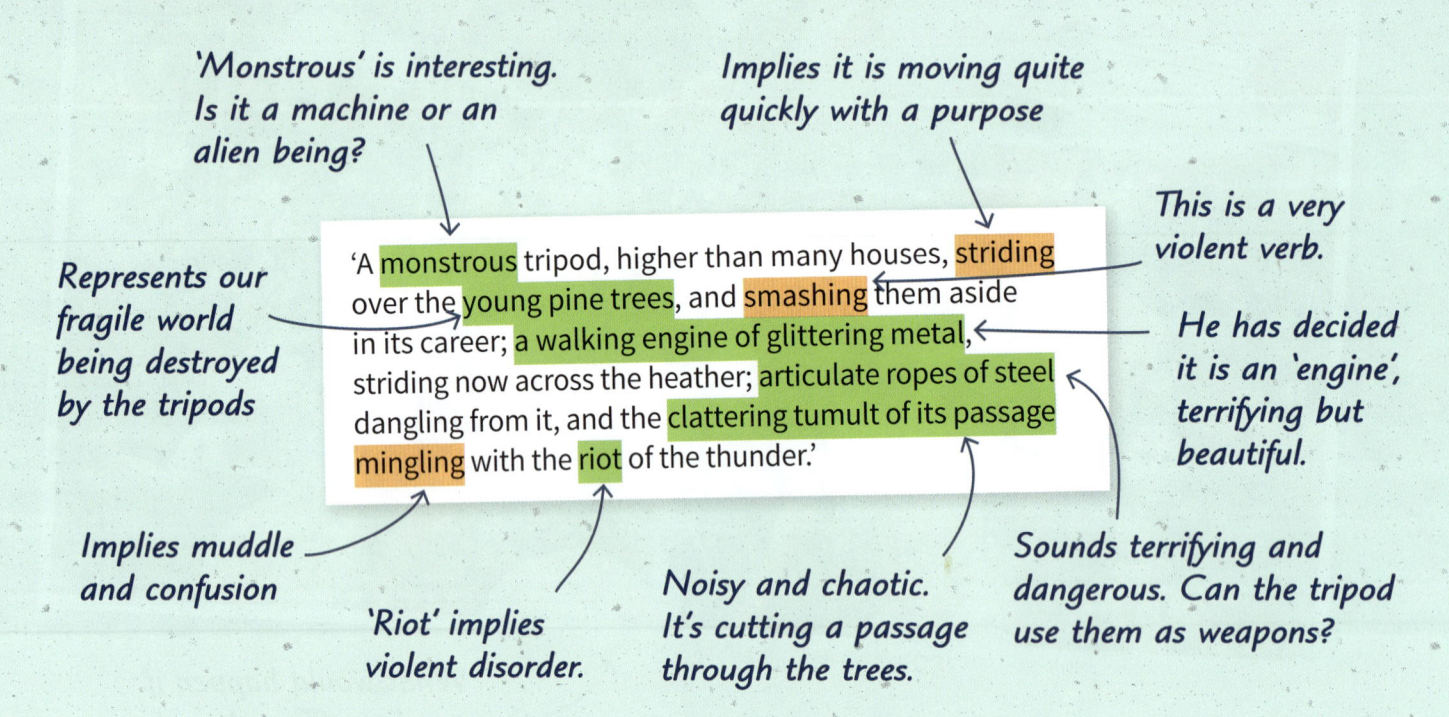

'Monstrous' is interesting. Is it a machine or an alien being?

Implies it is moving quite quickly with a purpose

Represents our fragile world being destroyed by the tripods

'A monstrous tripod, higher than many houses, striding over the young pine trees, and smashing them aside in its career; a walking engine of glittering metal, striding now across the heather; articulate ropes of steel dangling from it, and the clattering tumult of its passage mingling with the riot of the thunder.'

This is a very violent verb.

He has decided it is an 'engine', terrifying but beautiful.

Implies muddle and confusion

'Riot' implies violent disorder.

Noisy and chaotic. It's cutting a passage through the trees.

Sounds terrifying and dangerous. Can the tripod use them as weapons?

Now imagine a different kind of alien craft – a gigantic flying ship. Write a long sentence, like the example above, in which you describe what it is, what it looks like and what it does. You could start:

A gigantic flying ship, ...

> **Tip** ✅
>
> Look at how Wells uses semi-colons to break up the sentence.

Unit 3: Invasion!

2 The narrator compares the alien machines to everyday objects that would have been familiar to readers at that time, so they could visualise them. Re-read the following extract:

> 'Can you imagine a milking stool tilted and bowled violently along the ground? That was the impression those instant flashes gave. But instead of a milking stool imagine it a great body of machinery on a tripod stand.'

Notice how the narrator asks the reader a question, as if he's talking to us, checking that we understand. Try this for yourself.

Return to the alien craft you described in Activity 1. What everyday object could you use to help your readers visualise your spaceship? Make it an odd shape (for example, a pair of scissors or a seed from a tree) and use your ideas to write a paragraph using the same construction.

Can you imagine a... ?

Could a spaceship look like an everyday object or something in nature?

! Check your skills

Using the ideas you have already developed, write an episode describing an encounter with an alien ship as you are driving down a motorway. You should:

- create precise noun phrases to describe your spaceship
- choose your verbs carefully to describe what it does
- use comparisons with everyday objects to help readers visualise the spaceship.

Remember to check the grammar, spelling and punctuation of your final draft.

2.4 Chapter 2: Genres and themes

Unit 4

A touch of horror

In this unit, you will:

- Understand how a writer creates a feeling of unease through describing a setting.
- Explore how a writer creates **tension** through choosing effective verbs and nouns.
- Learn, understand and practise using new vocabulary.

Horror fiction has been sending shivers down our spines ever since it first appeared. We love books and films that scare us – perhaps because we know that it's all make-believe and no harm will really come to us. One important element of any horror story is the building of tension – the feeling we get when we know something awful is about to happen.

In his supernatural horror novel, *The Sacrifice Box*, Martin Stewart tells the story of five teenage friends who discover an ancient stone box hidden in a forest. One of the gang, 'Sep' Hope, has had a vision in which he was told what the gang must do with it. In the extract on page 57, the gang have carried out the instruction for each of them to place something important to them in the box.

Key term

tension a feeling of unease or nervousness when we know something important is about to happen

Ready, set, go!

As you read the extract opposite, look for the words and phrases that create tension.

56

Unit 4: A touch of horror

Extract from *The Sacrifice Box* by Martin Stewart
337 words

'Now what?' asked Arkle.

'We say Sep's words,' said Mack.

'They're not really mine,' said Sep, remembering how the words had come to him, like a knife driven into his skull – a waking dream so vivid he'd cried out in the bright sunshine.

'What do you mean?' said Lamb.

'I kind of dreamed them. They're just… they're the box's rules.'

'All right, so we say them. Then what?'

'Then we'll always be friends,' said Sep.

'How does *that* work?' said Arkle.

'Because we're making a promise to each other.'

[100 words] 'And it'll be *our* secret,' said Hadley, gripping her inhaler. 'We can't tell anyone.'

'Oh, I don't think we should talk about this at school,' said Arkle. 'I mean, it is kind of lame.'

The rain started again, cold drops on their hot skin. 'Let's say the words then,' Sep said. […]

They arranged themselves around the box as the rain grew heavier, draping the clearing's edge in grey sheets and closing them in.

Sep tried to peer through it.

Something was moving in the shadows between the trees.

He narrowed his eyes, focused on a shifting speck.

[200 words] There was a sound like someone whispering – or shouting from far away – and a long moment hung in the clearing. Sep **felt his skin crawl** as he sensed other figures around the box, their shadows closing in.

Then Hadley said, 'Sep?' and the moment lifted, and they were alone again.

Two **crows** spun through the rain. They settled on a branch high above them, shaking the drops from their feathers and shuffling their feet.

'I'm fine,' said Sep. […]

'Ready?' said Mack. 'Remember what to say?' Lamb nodded, her jaw muscles tight.

Something's really happening, Sep thought – then Hadley squeezed his hand, and he forgot about everything that wasn't her.

'Now,' she said. […]

[300 words] They spoke the words – the rules of the sacrifice. 'Never come to the box alone,' they said, hands unmoving.

'Never open it after dark,' they said, fingers joined together.
'Never take back your sacrifice,' they finished – then let go.

What sort of power might a stone box have?

---

felt his skin crawl – a common physical reaction to fear, which often features in horror stories

crows – black birds that live on carrion (dead animals) and are often seen as unlucky or linked with the supernatural

2.4 Chapter 2: Genres and themes

⚡ Word power

Re-read the extract on page 57. Pay particular attention to the target words listed below. As you read, think about what each of the words might mean in the extract.

Your target words for this section are:

- driven
- arranged
- draping
- sacrifice

These target words have been highlighted in blue in the extract on page 57.

1 We often think of driving in relation to a car but the word has a separate, related meaning. Look up 'driven' in the Target word list on pages 174–175. If you drive a nail into something, which of the following words best describe your action?

careful   forceful

accidental   fast

How would you describe driving a nail into something?

2 One meaning of the word 'arranged' is to put things in a neat or attractive order. Which one of the following activities might include arranging?

- Pouring milk onto cereal
- Putting candles on a birthday cake
- Scraping leftovers into the bin

Give reasons for your choice.

58

Unit 4: A touch of horror

3 The word 'draping' means covering or wrapping loosely with folds of cloth.

  a. In the extract, it is used to describe the way rain covers the landscape so that it can't be seen clearly. Which other kind of weather might 'drape' a landscape?

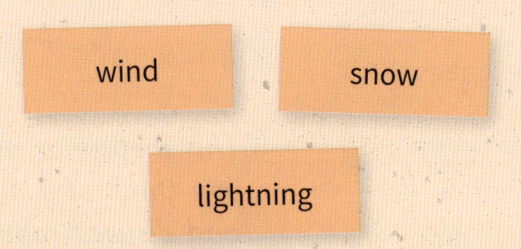

  wind   snow

  lightning

  b. Write a sentence using a form of the word 'drape' to describe a scene in that kind of weather.

  How do the rain and rain clouds remind you of something that drapes?

4 Look up the word 'sacrifice' in the Target word list on pages 174–175. Two definitions are given. Why do you think that Stewart might have intended us to give the word both meanings in the extract?

Knowledge and understanding

Look back at the extract on page 57 and answer the following questions.

1 Re-read the third paragraph. Which one of the statements below is true?

- Sep learned about the box during a nightmare.
- Hearing the instructions for the box caused Sep pain.
- Sep made up the rules for the box.

2 What is Sep told that putting the sacrifices into the box will do to the gang?

3 Explain in your own words why Arkle doesn't want to discuss the box at school.

4 Just before they say the words, Sep sees, hears and senses something.

  a. What does he see?

  b. What does he hear?

  c. What does he sense?

5 Sep and Hadley have a close relationship.

  a. What does she do just before they speak the words that tells us how she feels?

  b. What evidence is there that he has feelings for her?

59

2.4 Chapter 2: Genres and themes

📖 Reading skills

1 Not much happens during this extract but Stewart succeeds in creating tension. We feel that the box is supernatural – that it will have a terrible effect on the gang and that this is an important moment. So, how does he hint at this without saying it directly?

Re-read the section below, noticing how Stewart describes the weather to create a feeling of threat.

> 'The rain started again, cold drops on their hot skin. "Let's say the words then," Sep said.
> They arranged themselves around the box as the rain grew heavier, draping the clearing's edge in grey sheets and closing them in.'

- *The cold rain is a shock as it hits their hot skin.* → cold drops
- *It's raining harder now, suggesting it is more threatening.* → the rain grew heavier
- *This metaphor makes you think of a dusty old and disused room with the furniture covered in grey dust sheets.* → draping
- *It sounds as if they are trapped, like prisoners.* → closing them in

Use the annotations to help you write a paragraph explaining how Stewart uses language to create a threatening atmosphere.

2 Now look at how the extract continues. Sep is trying to identify something moving but he can't see it clearly because of the rain. This makes us want to find out too and so creates tension. Some nouns and noun phrases have been highlighted in green, the verbs in blue.

> 'Sep tried to peer through it.
> Something was moving in the shadows between the trees.
> He narrowed his eyes, focused on a shifting speck.'

- *Sep is making an effort but he still can't see clearly.* → tried to peer
- *Whatever it is, it's alive.* → Something was moving
- *It's too dark for him to see clearly.* → shadows
- *He doesn't know what it is. Neither do we.* → Something
- *More effort. We narrow our eyes when we are straining to see.* → narrowed
- *He is trying to see clearly, to bring the 'something' into focus to find out what it is.* → focused
- *It is still moving but it's tiny – a 'speck'.* → a shifting speck

60

Unit 4: A touch of horror

Notice how all the highlighted nouns are vague and don't give the thing a name, and the verbs are mostly physical, describing Sep straining to see.

Use the annotations and any ideas of your own to write a paragraph to explain how the writer creates tension in these lines. You could use some of the phrases on this page to introduce your ideas.

> The verb... makes us feel as if...

> This shows us that Sep is...

> The writer creates tension by...

> For example, when he says...

> The word... gives the impression that...

! Check your skills

Re-read the following section from the extract:

> 'There was a sound like someone whispering – or shouting from far away – and a long moment hung in the clearing. Sep felt his skin crawl as he sensed other figures around the box, their shadows closing in.'

Write your own commentary on how Stewart uses language to create a threatening atmosphere and to build up the tension in these lines.

Remember to focus on:
- the choices of verbs and nouns (especially vague nouns that don't name anything)
- descriptions of physical feelings.

Support your ideas with quotations from the text.

Do you think there were really other beings in the clearing?

61

2.5 Chapter 2: Genres and themes

Unit 5

A suspicious death

In this unit, you will:

- Understand how to use dialogue and description to establish character.
- Practise how to tell a story incorporating a range of verb tenses.
- Learn, understand and practise using new vocabulary.

The detective story is one of the most popular genres, and fictional detectives are among the best-known literary and TV characters. One reason for this is because the genre depends on strong characterisation. From Sherlock Holmes' sharp intelligence to Miss Marple's prim manner, writers give their fictional detectives recognisable characteristics to help readers to identify with them.

Another reason for the genre's success is that it gives readers the opportunity to solve a puzzle using clues from the case. If we solve it alongside the detective, we feel rather clever.

In the extract on page 63, from *The Christmas Card List* by Kate Ellis, Detective Inspector Wesley Peterson visits the scene of a poisoning.

Ready, set, go!

As you read the extract opposite, think about what you learn about Peterson from the way that he speaks and how he's described.

Unit 5: A suspicious death

Extract from *The Christmas Card List* by Kate Ellis
456 words

'Prudence Banks. Sixty five years old. Lived alone.' The constable studied his notebook as though he feared he'd missed something out.

'Who found her?' The speaker was a plain-clothes detective; dark-skinned with intelligent brown eyes. Detective Inspector Wesley Peterson was a good-looking man, although his unassuming manner suggested he was barely aware of the fact.

'The upstairs neighbours – James and Carla **Wordsworth**.'

'Like the poet?' Wesley said.

The constable, a new recruit who'd daydreamed his way through English Literature lessons at school, looked at his superior inquiringly.

Wesley studied his surroundings. The first-floor flat stood above a gallery on one of Tradmouth's main shopping streets; a **pedestrianised** thoroughfare where the shopfronts belied the **venerable** age of the buildings behind. In the smaller second-floor flat above lived the Wordsworths, Carla and James, who had found Miss Banks's body.

'Mr Wordsworth said the dead woman's radio was blasting out all night so first thing this morning he knocked on her door to make sure she was OK,' said the constable. 'When she didn't answer he was worried so he broke the door down. He found her like that.' He nodded towards the corpse. She'd clearly been sitting by the old-fashioned bureau, open to create a desk, then as death claimed her, she'd slumped off her chair onto the floor, a **grimace** of agony on her blue-tinged lips.

'Anyone back up his story?'

'His wife, Carla. And the next door neighbour heard the radio too. The walls are pretty thin.'

Wesley could see a pile of Christmas cards on the desk, a few were already sealed in neatly addressed envelopes, but the majority awaited a seasonal greeting from the deceased. The cards he could see bore a picture of an old stone house set in a large, snowy garden with a slightly sinister-looking robin in the foreground. The house looked familiar, but Wesley couldn't recall where he'd seen it before.

'Mr Wordsworth called the doctor but she'd obviously been dead some time,' the constable said. 'The doc suspected poisoning so he called us. Said he thought he could smell bitter almonds, whatever that means.'

Wesley heard a familiar voice outside on the landing. His boss, DCI Gerry Heffernan, was complaining about the cold weather in his loud, Liverpudlian accent. However, as soon as he entered he fell uncharacteristically silent and stopped in his tracks, staring at the dead woman.

'I know her,' he said after a few seconds. 'What's the story?'

Wesley tore his gaze away from the body. 'Locked room. Door bolted on the inside. Neighbour had to break in. Doctor suspected poisoning and called us.'

'Poisoning?' Gerry shook his head in disbelief. 'If it was, it must have been accidental. She's hardly the type to have enemies.'

Wordsworth – William Wordsworth (1770–1850) was a poet
pedestrianised – for walkers only; not for use by vehicles
venerable – old and respected
grimace – an ugly, twisted expression

2.5 Chapter 2: Genres and themes

⚡ Word power

Re-read the extract on page 63. Pay particular attention to the target words listed below. As you read, think about what each of the words might mean in the extract.

Your target words for this section are:

- unassuming
- inquiringly
- belied
- claimed
- uncharacteristically

These target words have been highlighted in blue in the extract on page 63.

Do you think the Christmas cards will be an important detail in the story?

1. The word 'unassuming' means modest. Use it in a paragraph describing a scientist who has been awarded a prize for inventing the cure for a fatal disease.

2. If you look at someone inquiringly, what are you most likely to say? Choose one of the following:

- 'No, thank you.'
- 'What do you mean?'
- 'Don't speak to me like that!'

Check the meaning in the Target word list on pages 174–175 to see if you are correct.

3. The word 'belied' means gave a false impression of something. Re-read where it is used in paragraph 6 of the extract and decide which of the following statements is true.

- The shops looked modern but were, in fact, old.
- The shops looked old but were, in fact, modern.

Unit 5: A suspicious death

4. One meaning of the word 'claimed' is 'said that one has a right to something'. Find it in the extract, where death is personified. Imagine the Grim Reaper standing before Prudence Banks and write a short scene describing the encounter and including the word 'claim'.

5. If someone behaves uncharacteristically, they are behaving in a way that is not typical of them. Remind yourself of Wesley Peterson's character and write a short paragraph in which you describe him acting or speaking 'uncharacteristically'.

Death is sometimes personified (made human) as the Grim Reaper cloaked in black and carrying a scythe.

Knowledge and understanding

Look back at the extract on page 63 and answer the following questions.

1. In the second paragraph, find three things that you learn about Detective Inspector Wesley Peterson.

2. Where do the Wordsworths live?

3. Re-read the paragraph beginning 'Mr Wordsworth said the dead woman's radio…' Using information in this paragraph, decide which of the following statements are probably true.
   - Prudence Banks died in the evening.
   - She struggled with her killer.
   - She was writing when she died.
   - She was listening to the radio when she was killed.

4. Re-read the paragraph beginning 'Wesley could see…' What was Prudence Banks doing when she was killed?

5. Re-read the paragraph beginning 'Wesley heard a familiar voice…' What two things do we learn about DCI Gerry Heffernan in this paragraph?

6. At the end of the extract, DCI Gerry Heffernan says, 'She's hardly the type to have enemies.' What might cause him to think that?

2.5 Chapter 2: Genres and themes

✏️ Writing skills

1 Look at how Ellis uses dialogue and description to:
- inform the reader of the facts of the case
- convey information about the characters of the detective and the constable, and their relationship.

Wesley is the senior officer. He asks a direct, business-like question.

Describes his physical appearance and personality

> '"Who found her?" The speaker was a plain-clothes detective; dark-skinned with intelligent brown eyes. Detective Inspector Wesley Peterson was a good-looking man, although his unassuming manner suggested he was barely aware of the fact.
>
> "The upstairs neighbours – James and Carla Wordsworth."
>
> "Like the poet?" Wesley said.'

Gives straightforward information, which may turn out to be important later

He is well-educated and has a sense of humour.

a. Re-read the next paragraph in the extract. What do we learn about the constable and how does he compare to Wesley?

b. Find two more pieces of dialogue from later in the extract that inform the reader about the known facts of the case.

Key terms

past perfect progressive tense made up of 'had' and 'been' and the present participle of the verb (ending '-ing'). It is used for something that started happening in the past and was still happening at a later time, e.g. *They had been training for the tournament for months*

past perfect tense made with 'had' plus the past participle of the verb (often ending '-ed'). It indicates that an action was completed at some point in the past before something else happened, e.g. *I had just returned when the phone rang*

past tense used to describe things that have already happened

simple past tense often ends '-ed' and is used for something that happened in the past and is now finished, e.g. *He jumped the queue*

Unit 5: A suspicious death

2 Look at the sentence on the right, in which Wesley imagines the woman's death based on evidence from the crime scene.

The writer has used three different **past tenses** to guide us through Wesley's version of the events leading to the victim's death. She has also included a great deal of descriptive information, punctuated by commas to help us imagine the scene vividly.

Create a similarly structured sentence about a scientist who was shot in a laboratory while carrying out an experiment. Include:

- three different past tenses to describe the events
- descriptive detail punctuated by commas to help readers imagine the murder
- a striking final image.

past perfect progressive tense

'She'd clearly been sitting by the old fashioned bureau, open to create a desk, then as death claimed her, she'd slumped off her chair onto the floor, a grimace of agony on her blue-tinged lips.'

past perfect tense   *simple past tense*

! Check your skills

Will your detective be similar or very different from Sherlock?

Using the extract as a model, write the opening of a detective story in which the murder victim has been found dead in the kitchen. It seems they were making dinner because the cooker was still on and the smoke alarm ringing. Make your detective a confident middle-aged woman.

End your writing with a sentence in which the detective imagines the murder based on the evidence of the crime scene.

Remember to include:

- dialogue and description to convey characters and facts about the case
- a range of past tenses to guide your reader through the known and imagined events surrounding the murder.

Check your final draft for grammar, spelling and punctuation errors.

67

2.6 Chapter 2: Genres and themes

Unit 6
Writing assessment

Think back over the extracts you have read in this chapter. Remind yourself of the vocabulary and writing techniques you have learned. Now it's time for you to put your skills into practice as you complete your own writing task.

Choose one of the writing tasks below to complete. Each one asks you to tackle a different genre. Whichever one you select, you should follow the same process below.

1. Remind yourself of the features of the appropriate genre that you explored during the chapter. Then plan your writing with those features in mind, jotting ideas down as bullet points or in a spider diagram.

2. Try to use some of the target words in this chapter, but remember to use them correctly.

3. Write your first draft. Try to make your writing as good as it can be, but remember that you will have the chance to revise and improve it.

4. Edit your draft.
   - Check you have used at least some of the techniques you have learned about.
   - Check your spelling and punctuation.

5. Write a final version ready for assessment.

Tip

It is often helpful to read your work aloud when you are editing or proofreading.

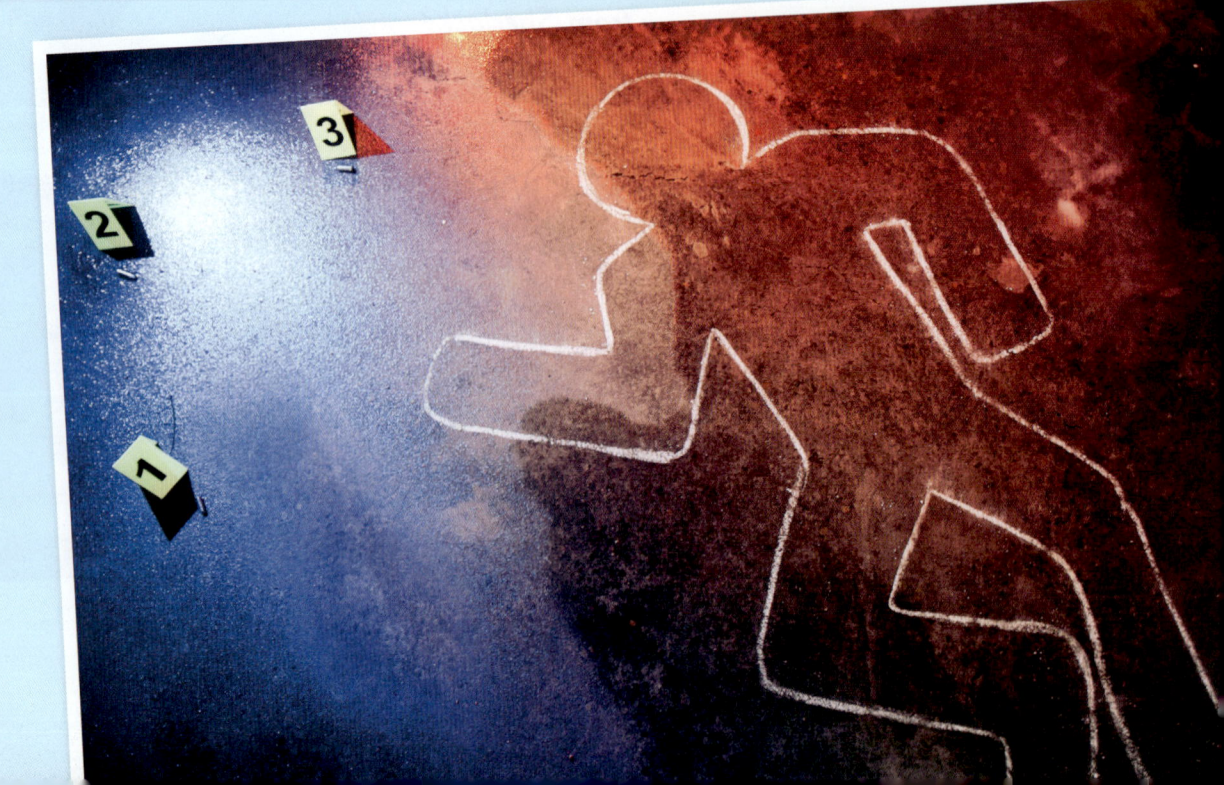

Unit 6: Writing assessment

Choose **one** of the following writing tasks:

Task A

Return to the magical character you created in response to Terry Pratchett's writing in Unit 1. Continue the story, following the character's day. Think about how your character will use their magical power and what effect it has on others. Does their family know about the power or has your character kept it hidden? You should:

- remember to keep your character's personality consistent as you write
- include references to the object that represents your character's powers (like Tiffany's hat)
- remember that your character is still learning how to use their powers so something could go wrong.

Task B

Return to the extract from *The Sacrifice Box* on page 57 and continue the story for a page. Focus on what might happen to Sep and the others immediately after they carry out the ceremony at the box. Sep senses 'other figures' around them. Don't reveal who or what they are but think about how they might react to the ceremony. You should:

- aim to maintain the feeling of tension through language describing the weather and the setting
- think about how the unseen forces that govern the sacrifice box might respond to the teenagers' actions
- remember to focus on Sep as the main character but bring in some of the others by giving them dialogue or significant actions.

Task C

Return to your writing about the crime scene based on your reading of *The Christmas Card List* on page 63. Continue your writing to describe what happens as your detective examines the crime scene more closely. Remember, your murder victim has been found dead in the kitchen as they were making dinner, the cooker was still on and the smoke alarm ringing. You should:

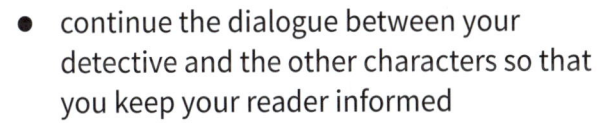

- continue the dialogue between your detective and the other characters so that you keep your reader informed
- continue to develop your detective's character through description and dialogue
- use varied forms of the past tense to ensure that the retelling of events is clear
- bring a senior officer to the scene. What sort of character are they? How will your detective react to them?

What clues might your detective find?

3 People and voices

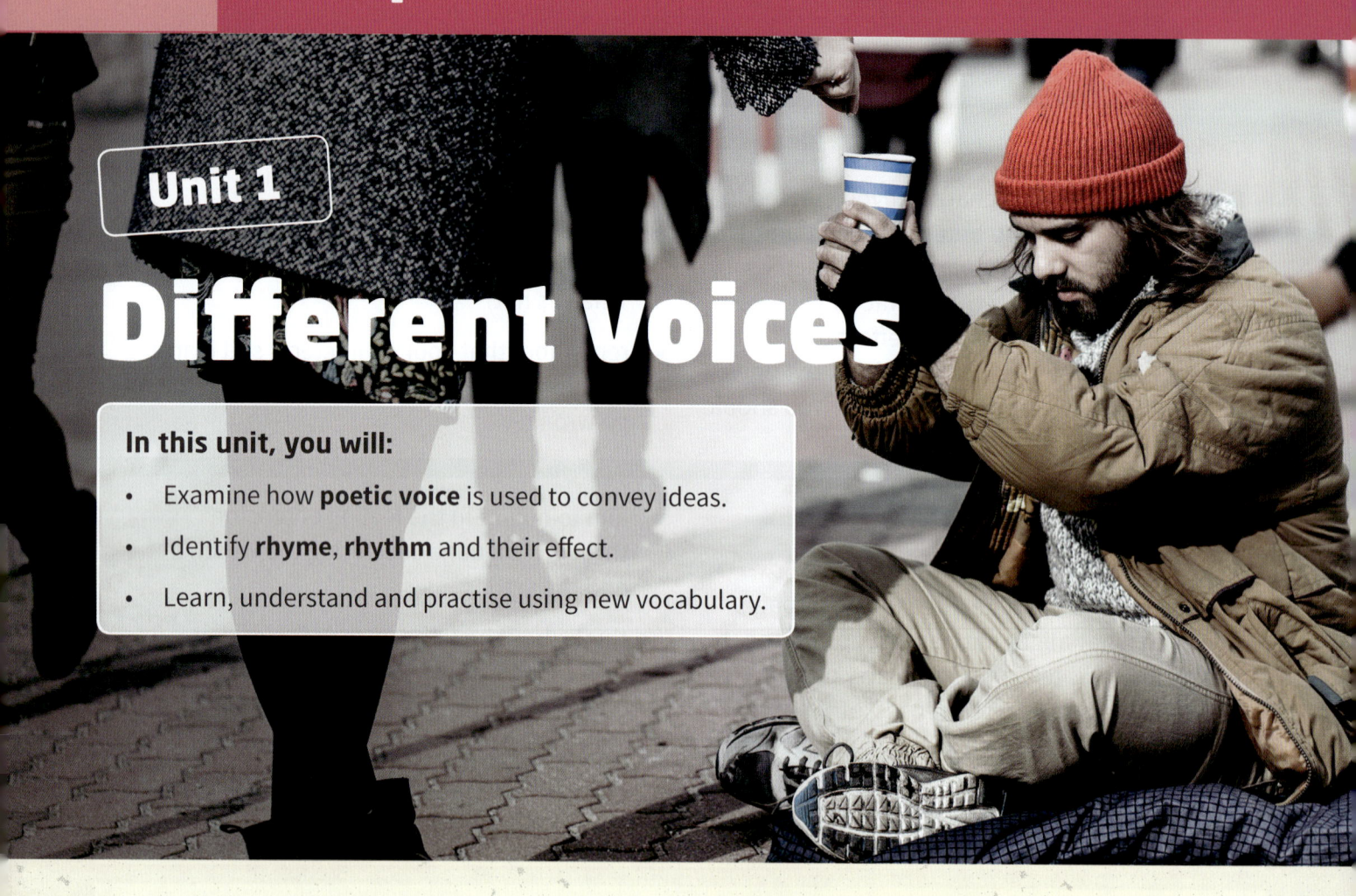

Unit 1
Different voices

In this unit, you will:
- Examine how **poetic voice** is used to convey ideas.
- Identify **rhyme**, **rhythm** and their effect.
- Learn, understand and practise using new vocabulary.

Reading poetry is not a silent activity. Poetry should be read aloud. Without hearing poetry, we can miss the sounds, patterns and rhythms that poets have carefully crafted. The poems in this chapter will introduce you to these important aspects of poetry. You will also hear a range of different voices. Sometimes the voice might be the poet's own. Sometimes the poets take on the voices of other people, or even use their imagination to create the voices of inanimate things.

In the poem on page 71 the poet takes on the voice of a homeless person living on the streets.

Key terms

poetic voice the voice conveyed by a poem. This could be the poet's own voice or an imagined persona

rhyme the same sound used in words or the endings of words, especially at the ends of lines of poetry

rhythm the pattern made by the 'beats' in language or music

Ready, set, go!

As you read, think about the impression you get of the homeless person from the way their voice is presented in the poem.

Unit 1: Different voices

'Give' by Simon Armitage
83 words

Of all the public places, dear
To make a scene, I've chosen here.

Of all the doorways in the world
To choose to sleep, I've chosen yours.
I'm on the street, under the stars.

For **coppers** I can dance or sing.
For silver – swallow swords, eat fire.
For gold – escape from locks and chains.

It's not as if I'm holding out
For **frankincense** or **myrrh**, just change.

You give me tea. That's big of you.
I'm on my knees. I beg of you.

---

coppers – low value British money
frankincense, myrrh – gifts given in the biblical story of the three kings at the birth of Jesus

3.1 Chapter 3: People and voices

⚡ Word power

Re-read the poem on page 71. Pay particular attention to the target words and phrases listed below. As you read, think about the way the narrator might say these words. What **tone** of voice is appropriate?

Your target words for this section are:

- public
- make a scene
- holding out
- that's big of you

These target words have been highlighted in blue in the poem on page 71.

What do you think of when you hear the word 'public'?

1. Use the Target word list on pages 174–175 to check the meaning of the word 'public'.

   a. Explain in your own words the difference between public and private.

   b. What does the word 'public' suggest about the life of this homeless person?

2. The phrase 'make a scene' has a double meaning in this poem.

   a. Look at the two meanings of the phrase below. Armitage plays with both meanings in this poem. Explain how both meanings are relevant to the situation presented in this poem:

   - Make a scene – create a setting or something to be looked at by other people. For example, the window dressers made a beautiful winter scene in the December shop window.

   - Make a scene – to cause a problem by creating a disturbance in public. For example, the toddler made a scene in the restaurant after she dropped her ice cream.

   b. Write two sentences of your own using the phrase 'make a scene'. Use the phrase with a different meaning in each sentence.

Unit 1: Different voices

3. The phrase 'holding out' has two meanings:
   - to hold in your hand and offer outwards. For example, he held out his ticket to the ticket collector.
   - to delay or wait for something. For example, she was holding out for the job in the bank, so she didn't accept the first offer she received from the accountancy firm.

   Look carefully at the use of this phrase in the poem. Which meaning is the poet using, or is it both? Give reasons for your answer.

4. The phrase 'that's big of you' can be used to suggest someone is being generous. It can also be used sarcastically to suggest that someone is making a gesture of being generous but that it is not good enough. The speaker might be presented as sarcastic or critical of the person he is speaking to at this point in the poem. Explain why this might be the case.

Key terms

stanza a verse of poetry

tone how a writer's or speaker's attitude to the subject matter is expressed, e.g. an angry or concerned or polite tone

Knowledge and understanding

1. From the first two **stanzas**, what do you know about where the speaker has decided to stay for the night?

2. Who is the homeless person speaking to? What information are we given about the person the poem addresses?

Tip

Not much is revealed about them, so be careful to only use the evidence from the poem rather than your own imagination.

3. What does the speaker want from the person he is speaking to?

4. Explain why the speaker thinks there could be a need to sing, dance or entertain others.

5. The Christian Christmas story about the birth of Jesus is a story about a desperate family looking for kindness and a place to rest. This is not a religious poem but it does draw on images from that well-known story.

   a. What images in this poem link to the Christmas story?

   b. Why do you think Armitage echoes this story in his portrayal of a modern homeless person?

3.1 Chapter 3: People and voices

✏️ Writing skills

1 Armitage uses a gentle even rhythm to portray the homeless person in a gentle compassionate way.

   a. Read the two lines below aloud.

   > Of **all** the **pub**lic **pla**ces, **dear**
   > To **make** a **scene**, I've **cho**sen **her**e.

   - Find the two rhyming words. In which lines of the poem are they found?
   - Notice the use of four heavy rhythmic beats in each line (underlined and in bold). Emphasise these sounds when you read aloud.

   b. Write another two lines, keeping to the same rhyme pattern and rhythm, to describe a homeless person's situation. An example first line is given below for you to complete, or you can write your own two lines.

   > *Despite the cold and all my fear,*
   > _____.

   Read it aloud and check you have two rhyming words and four heavy rhythmic beats in each line.

2 A poet's choice of words can create a specific tone for the poetic voice they present in a poem. For example, certain words or phrases might create a gentle or sympathetic tone.

   a. Look at the following student's comment on the tone they think is created in the opening of the poem and explain whether you agree with this.

   > *'Of all the public places, dear': the opening of the poem sounds like someone talking. The word 'dear' sounds gentle in the way a kind person might talk to someone they know. This makes the homeless person sound gentle rather than threatening.*

   b Find another quotation from the opening of the poem that you think helps to create a gentle or sympathetic tone.

Unit 1: **Different voices**

3 Now re-read the final stanza where the speaker of the poem emphasises the contrast between themselves and those who are not living on the streets.

> You give me tea. That's big of you.
> I'm on my knees. I beg of you.

Think about the poetic voice in this stanza. What tone do you think is created here? Remember to select quotations and comment on how the poet creates this tone through his choice of words.

How do their lives compare?

! Check your skills

Use the lines in Activity 3 above as a model to write your own two lines that contrast the homeless with people that live more comfortable lives.

Try to keep the poetic voice, rhyme pattern and rhythm the same as the poet's.

3.2 Chapter 3: People and voices

Unit 2
Serious comedy

In this unit, you will:
- Understand and compare how humour is used to convey a writer's concerns.
- Analyse the effects of **repetition** in poetry.
- Learn, understand and practise using new vocabulary.

The poem on page 77 is a humorous poem with a serious message about our political leaders. It is written by the Afro-Guyanese poet John Agard. He performs his poems in a fun and energetic way, using humour to entertain as well as make us think about bigger issues.

Key term

repetition repeating a term or idea more than once

Ready, set, go!

As you read the poem opposite, notice the repetition of the first two lines and the important messages in the final two lines of each stanza.

Unit 2: **Serious comedy**

'Crybaby Prime Minister' by John Agard
156 words

I'd love to be led
by a crybaby prime minister
who'd burst into tears
whenever people bled

I'd love to be led
by a crybaby prime minister
who'd sob and sob
for everyone without a job

I'd love to be led
by a crybaby prime minister
who'd lose all control
when told of old folks in the cold

I'd love to be led
by a crybaby prime minister
who'd whimper for a while
at the mention of **nuclear missile**

I'd love to be led
by a crybaby prime minister
who'd suddenly weep
for children with nowhere to sleep

I'd love to be led
by a crybaby prime minister
whose eyes would go red
when trees of the forest are felled

Yes, there's something to be said
for a nation being led
by a crybaby prime minister
who'd reach for a hanky
with a lump in the throat

Such a prime minister
might be worth a vote.

---

nuclear missile – powerful weapon of mass destruction

3.2 Chapter 3: People and voices

⚡ Word power

Re-read the poem on page 77. Pay particular attention to the target words listed below. As you read, think about what each of the words might mean in this context and how they help to suggest Agard's views about politicians.

Your target words for this section are:

- whimper
- mention
- felled
- nation

These target words have been highlighted in blue in the text on page 77.

How could you use the word 'felled' to describe what happened here?

1. Agard creates humour by using words in relation to a prime minister that seem inappropriate for a person with such power. The word 'whimper' means to cry softly and we usually associate it with something small or powerless.

Write two sentences that use this word more typically, for example:

The toddler whimpered as he tried to pull his arm from the railings.

2. The word 'mention' can be used as a noun or a verb.

He mentioned that he was feeling nervous. (verb)

The mention of chocolate made his stomach rumble. (noun)

a. Write your own two sentences. In the first, use 'mention' as a verb. In the second, use 'mention' as a noun.

b. Look back at the poem. Is the word 'mention' used as a verb or a noun?

Unit 2: Serious comedy

3 The word 'felled' means knocked or chopped down.

  a. Re-read stanza 6 of the poem. Why do you think Agard has chosen to use the more unusual word 'felled' in line 24 instead of 'chopped down'?

  b. The word 'felled' is sometimes used in writing about sport. Look at the image on page 78 and write a sentence using the word 'felled' to describe the picture.

4 Look up the word 'nation' in the Target word list on pages 174–175. Write down as many other words as you can that contain the word 'nation', for example:

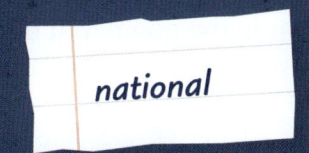

national

Knowledge and understanding

1 Re-read stanza 1 of the poem. Which explanation below best fits your reading of Agard's message in this stanza?

He would like a prime minister who:
- would be upset if anyone cut themselves
- would be upset at the suffering of other people
- could not stand the sight of blood
- would cry if they were injured.

2 What does Agard mean when he says he thinks a good prime minister would do the following?

'lose all control when told of old folks in the cold'

3 What does the word 'led' in the quotation below suggest about the relationship between a prime minister and the people?

'I'd love to be led…'

4 Which adjectives best describe what Agard thinks a good prime minister should be like? Write a paragraph to explain your choice, using quotations from the text to support your view. Choose your own word or use the list below for ideas.

kind   emotional   organised

uncontrolled   compassionate   childish

Should a prime minister care about older people not being able to afford to keep warm in winter?

79

3.2 Chapter 3: People and voices

Reading skills

1 a. Agard uses humorous, childish language in his poem. Identify three quotations in the poem that demonstrate childish language, for example:

> 'who'd sob and sob'

b. Now use your quotations to explain how the poet combines humorous and serious ideas to convey his views about politicians. You might like to use the same sentence starters (underlined) as in the example below.

> 'who'd sob and sob' – <u>This creates humour because</u> the idea that a politician might cry is surprising and because of the repetition of the simple word 'sob'. <u>Agard uses it to make a serious point that</u> politicians should be more caring and affected by the problems of the world.

2 Some poems or songs include a line (or set of lines) that is repeated regularly. This repeated line is called a refrain. The **structure** of this poem relies on a refrain.

a. What is the refrain in this poem?

b. People often repeat a message to emphasise its importance. What important message is the poet trying to emphasise in his refrain? Explain it using your own words.

3 As you listen carefully to the poem being read, look at its shape on the page. Agard changes the verse structure to emphasise a key message. This changes the pace and rhythm of the poem.

a. Where does this happen?

b. What message does it draw our attention to?

> **Key term**
>
> **structure** how a text is ordered, the connections made between ideas and themes, and where the writer is directing the reader's focus

80

Unit 2: Serious comedy

4 The final two lines of the poem sit alone. Select the three most useful statements below to reflect Agard's ideas in the final lines.

- It would make a change to have a prime minister who is compassionate or emotional.
- He does not vote in elections for prime ministers.
- It would be unusual to have a prime minister with feelings.
- It would be worth having a prime minister with feelings.
- There has never been a kind prime minister.

How would you react to seeing a politician crying?

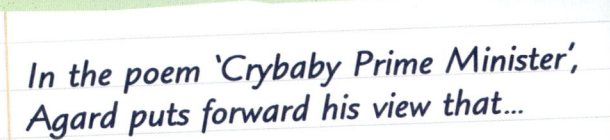

Check your skills

Write a paragraph explaining how Agard uses language and structure to convey his views about political leaders. Consider the following aspects and their effects on readers:

- humour
- refrain and repetition
- verse structure and the poem's ending.

You might like to use the sentence starters on the right.

In the poem 'Crybaby Prime Minister', Agard puts forward his view that…

He uses humour to convey his serious message via his unusual language choices, for example…

He uses repetition to… For example…

He uses structure to convey his message by changing his verse structures at the end of the poem…

3.3 Chapter 3: People and voices

Unit 3
Changing identity

In this unit, you will:

- Understand how **contrast** can be used to convey personal experience.
- Explore the effect of **personification** in poetic and descriptive writing.
- Learn, understand and practise using new vocabulary.

Have you ever moved from one place to another and had to adapt? The poem on page 83 is by the Scottish poet Jackie Kay. The speaker in the poem describes an experience of moving from Scotland and losing the sounds and words of her Scottish voice.

Ready, set, go!

As you read the extract opposite, listen to how the poet combines contrasting words from **standard English** with the words and sounds of Scotland. You don't need to understand the meaning of every individual word in order to understand the poem.

Key terms

contrast a comparison of two things to show their differences

personification representing an idea in human form or a thing as having human characteristics

standard English the English taught in schools and used in most books, newspapers and formal documents

Unit 3: Changing identity

'Old Tongue' by Jackie Kay
208 words

When I was eight, I was forced south.
Not long after, when I opened
my mouth, a strange thing happened.
I lost my Scottish accent.
Words fell off my tongue:
eedyit, *dreich*, *wabbit*, *crabbit*,
stummer, *teuchter*, *heidbanger*,
so you are, *so am ur*, *see you*, *see ma ma*,
shut yer geggie or I'll gie you the malkie!

My own **vowels** started to stretch like my bones
and I **turned my back on** Scotland.
Words disappeared in the dead of night,
new words marched in: ghastly, awful,
quite dreadful, *scones* said like *stones*.
Pokey hats into ice-cream cones.
Oh where did all my words go –
my old words, my lost words?
Did you ever feel sad when you lost a word,
did you ever try and call it back
like calling in the sea?
If I could have found my words wandering,
I swear I would have taken them in,
swallowed them whole, **knocked them back**.

Out in the English soil, my old words
buried themselves. It made my mother's blood boil.
I cried one day with the wrong sound in my mouth.
I wanted them back; I wanted my old accent back,
my old tongue. My dour, **soor** Scottish tongue.
Sing-songy. I wanted to *gie it laldie*.

---

vowels – the letters a, e, i, o, u and their sounds
turned my back on – rejected
knocked them back – gulped them down
soor – sour
gie it laldie – to do it with energy

Do you call ice cream cones 'pokey hats', or something else entirely?

83

3.3 Chapter 3: People and voices

⚡ Word power

Re-read the poem on page 83. Pay particular attention to the target words and **phrases** listed below. As you read, think about how they help you understand the speaker's experience and feelings about her old way of speaking.

Your target words and phrases for this section are:

- accent
- wandering
- made my… blood boil
- dour

These target words and phrases have been highlighted in blue in the text on page 83.

1 Look up the meaning of the word 'wandering' in the Target word list on pages 174–175. What does it suggest about how the speaker imagines her words are feeling and behaving?

2 Look at the following definitions of the word 'accent':

- a way of pronouncing (speaking) words, especially one associated with a particular country, area or social class
- emphasis on one word, sound or letter in speech.

Which definition best fits the speaker's use of the word 'accent' in line 4 of the poem?

3 The target phrase 'made my blood boil' is used **figuratively** rather than literally.

Read the phrase below and its literal and figurative meanings.

my voice broke –
my voice stopped working (literal meaning)
my voice got deeper as part of adolescence (figurative meaning)

Now write the literal meaning and the figurative meaning for the target phrase 'made my blood boil'.

Key terms

figuratively used imaginatively to convey an idea, often in the form of a comparison

phrase a group of words that forms a unit

Unit 3: Changing identity

4 The word 'dour' means stern or gloomy in looks or manner, for example:

> *She became dour and withdrawn when she lived on her own.*

Think of someone you know who might be described as 'dour'. They could be a fictional character or a celebrity. Write a sentence about them, using their name and the word 'dour'.

> *Craig Revel Horwood is famous for looking dour on Strictly Come Dancing.*

Knowledge and understanding

1 When did the speaker in the poem move south from Scotland?

2 When the speaker moved, they stopped using many Scottish words and phrases. Which lines of the poem list the words and phrases that they no longer use?

3 Kay uses personification in the line 'new words marched in…' The speaker describes the words as if they are alive, like a person. Find another example of personification in the poem.

4 Re-read stanza 2 of the poem.

  a. Copy and complete the list on the right of ways that the speaker's language changed.

  b. How did the speaker feel about losing her words?

  c. How did the speaker's mother feel about the changed voice?

> *She gained new words such as ………, ……… and ghastly.*

> *She changed the way she said 'scone', so that it rhymed with ……….*

> *She stopped saying 'pokey hats' and instead called them ……….*

85

3.3 Chapter 3: People and voices

✏️ Writing skills

1 Kay uses contrasting words in her poem to reflect a change in the speaker's life.

  a. Think about two school settings you have experienced, for example your current school and a previous one. Create a word bank that contains contrasting words to reflect the differences between each place and your feelings about each of them. Use a table like the one below, placing the school names at the left of each row.

  b. Look back at Kay's use of personification in the poem. Use the same method to write a sentence about your feelings about each of the places in your table.

School 1

School 2

Unit 3: Changing identity

2 Everyone has a range of vocabulary, some of which is linked to their own personal interests, situation or experiences. For example:
- You may use words and phrases that older people rarely use or understand.
- You may have lived in different places where some words and phrases are used differently.
- You may be interested in a sport or activity that has its own specialist language.
- Your family may have particular words and phrases or nicknames from your early childhood that you use just among your family.

a. Write a bank of words that are particular to you, linked to your personal interests and experiences.

b. Write a short paragraph about some of the words in your word bank, explaining why these words are particular to your personal identity.

! Check your skills

Think about a time when you have experienced a change in your life, for example moving to a new home, moving schools or gaining a new friend or family member. Choose one of the tasks below to check your skills.

- Write two paragraphs to describe 'before' and 'after' that change in your life.
- Write a poem using two stanzas, one focusing on before the change and one after.

For whichever task you choose:
- Bring out the differences before and after the change by thinking about contrasts.
- Describe how your words changed to reflect the change in your life. If possible, use personification to describe the change in your language.
- Give your work a title.
- Check your work carefully for accuracy with spelling, grammar and punctuation.

3.4 Chapter 3: People and voices

Unit 4
Persuasive voices

In this unit, you will:
- Identify **figurative language** and consider its effects.
- Consider Shakespeare's use of language and what it conveys about character and relationships.
- Learn, understand and practise using new vocabulary.

The extract on page 89 is from Shakespeare's play *Macbeth*. The king of Scotland is staying in Macbeth's castle. Macbeth and his wife are discussing a plan to kill him so that Macbeth can become king himself. Macbeth is reluctant at first, but Lady Macbeth is very persuasive.

Key term

figurative language words or expressions with a meaning that is different from the literal meaning

Ready, set, go!

As you read the extract opposite, think about the contrasting opinions of Macbeth and Lady Macbeth at the beginning of this conversation and how Macbeth's opinion changes.

Unit 4: Persuasive voices

Extract from *Macbeth,* Act 1 Scene 7 by William Shakespeare
323 words

Macbeth We will proceed no further in this business.
He hath **honoured me of late**, and I have bought
Golden opinions from all sorts of people,
Which would be worn now in their newest gloss,
Not cast aside so soon.

honoured me of late – given me respect or honours recently

Lady Macbeth   Was the hope drunk *(Line 5)*
Wherein you dressed yourself? Hath it slept since?
And wakes it now, to look so green and pale
At what it did so freely? From this time
Such I **account** thy love. Art thou **afeard**
To be the same in thine own **act and valour** *(Line 10)*
As thou art in desire? Wouldst thou have that
Which thou esteem'st the **ornament of life**,
And live a coward in thine own esteem,
Letting 'I dare not' wait upon 'I would',
Like the **poor cat i'th'adage**? *(Line 15)*

account – value
afeard – afraid
act and valour – actions and bravery

ornament of life – the king's crown

poor cat i'th'adage – like the poor cat who would like to eat fish but wouldn't get its paws wet

(…)

Macbeth If we should fail?

Lady Macbeth   We fail?
But **screw your courage to the sticking-place**
And we'll not fail. When Duncan is asleep,
Whereto the rather shall **his day's hard journey**
Soundly invite him, his two **chamberlains** *(Line 20)*
Will I with wine and **wassail** so convince,
That memory, the **warder** of the brain,
Shall be a **fume**, and the receipt of reason
A **limbeck** only. When in swinish sleep
Their drenchèd natures lies as in a death, *(Line 25)*
What cannot you and I perform upon
Th'unguarded Duncan? What not put upon
His **spongy** officers, who shall bear the guilt
Of our great **quell**?

screw your courage to the sticking-place – be brave
his day's hard journey / Soundly invite him – after a tiring day he will want to sleep
chamberlains – king's officers
wassail – spicy wine or partying
warder – guardian
fume – like smoke or gas
limbeck – an instrument used in purifying liquids

spongy – soaked in drink
quell – killing, murder

Macbeth   Bring forth men-children only,
For thy undaunted mettle should **compose** *(Line 30)*
Nothing but males. Will it not be **received**,
When we have marked with blood those sleepy two
Of his own chamber and used their very daggers,
That they have done't?

compose – produce
received – believed

Lady Macbeth   Who dares receive it other,
As we shall make our griefs and clamour roar *(Line 35)*
Upon his death?

Macbeth   I am **settled**, and bend up
Each **corporal agent** to this terrible feat.
Away, and **mock the time with fairest show**.
False face must hide what the false heart doth know.

settled – decided
corporal agent – body part
mock the time with fairest show – pretend everything is normal

89

3.4 Chapter 3: People and voices

⚡ Word power

Re-read the extract on page 89. Pay particular attention to the target words listed below. As you read, think about what each word might mean in context.

Your target words for this section are:

- drenched
- perform
- undaunted
- clamour

These target words have been highlighted in blue in the extract on page 89.

Everything in the car was absolutely drenched!

1

a. Look up the word 'drenched' in the Target word list on pages 174–175. Then look at the words below. Put each word in the most appropriate place on a line like the one below.

damp   drenched   soaking   dripping   soggy

Least wet   **Most wet**

1   2   3   4   5

b. Complete the sentences below, using the most appropriate word from the list above.

After being caught in a severe storm, I was _____.

The toddler shook his bottle of milk and his cot was _____.

Unit 4: Persuasive voices

2 The verb 'perform' can be used to mean:
- to carry out or to do something
- to act publicly for entertainment, such as on a stage.

Look back at line 26 of the text. Which meaning is appropriate when Lady Macbeth talks about what they will do to the king? Explain your answer.

3 The word 'undaunted' suggests that someone is brave and determined when faced with difficult circumstances.

Write a sentence about a time when you or someone you know was brave when facing a large or small difficulty. Use the word 'undaunted' in your sentence, for example:

Eleanor was undaunted as she walked through the school gates, despite the group of gossiping girls standing nearby.

4 Lady Macbeth describes how she and Macbeth will behave to make everyone think they are upset:

> 'As we shall make our griefs and clamour roar
> Upon his death'

What does the word 'clamour' suggest about the way they will behave? Use the Target word list on pages 174–175 if you need to.

How does Lady Macbeth persuade her husband?

Knowledge and understanding

1 Identify and copy out the line that suggests that at first Macbeth does not want to carry out the plan to kill King Duncan.

2 a. In lines 5–15, Lady Macbeth is scornful that her husband does not dare to act. Explain how she tries to make him feel bad when she says:

> 'From this time
> Such I account thy love.'

Use the glossary to help you.

b. Re-read lines 9–15. Using a quotation from the text, explain how Lady Macbeth tries to make her husband change his mind.

3 Write a list of four actions in the Macbeths' plan (lines 19–33). The first one is:

Check Duncan is asleep.

91

3.4 Chapter 3: People and voices

Reading skills

What kind of relationship do you think Macbeth and his wife have?

1. **Metaphor** and personification are forms of figurative language. In lines 3–5, Macbeth uses an **extended metaphor** to describe how he would like to enjoy the 'golden opinions' that people currently have of him.

   > 'Golden opinions from all sorts of people,
   > Which would be worn now in their newest gloss,
   > Not cast aside so soon.'

   a. In your own words, explain what he means. You could begin:

   > In these lines, Macbeth suggests that he does not want to kill King Duncan because…

   b. Complete the sentence below to explain how the metaphor creates an interesting image for the audience.

   > He describes the opinions of others as though they are…

Key terms

extended metaphor a lengthy description that describes something as something else in order to create a vivid picture in the reader's mind

metaphor describing something as something else, not meant to be taken literally, e.g. *You are a star*

Unit 4: Persuasive voices

2 In lines 6–8, Lady Macbeth uses personification to convey her view about Macbeth changing his mind about killing Duncan to achieve his own hopes of being king.

   a. Re-read the quotation below. Which quality is Lady Macbeth personifying?

> 'Was the hope drunk
> Wherein you dressed yourself? Hath it slept since?
> And wakes it now, to look so green and pale
> At what it did so freely?'

   b. Re-read Macbeth's extended metaphor in lines 3–5. What is similar about the way Macbeth and Lady Macbeth are using language (including figurative language)? Explain this in your own words, using quotations to support your points.

   c. Why do you think Lady Macbeth links Macbeth with 'green and pale'? What does this convey about her view of his behaviour?

   d. Why do you think Shakespeare chooses similar language methods for this married couple? What does it suggest about them and their relationship? Explain this in your own words, using quotations to support your points.

! Check your skills

Re-read the last six lines of the extract. Consider the language of Macbeth and his wife as they decide how to act in order that the king's guards will be blamed for his murder.

- Explain what the pair will do to ensure they are not blamed.
- Identify a metaphor they use to convey how they will behave.
- Use your own words to explain what it suggests about the way they will behave.

93

3.5 Chapter 3: People and voices

Unit 5
Reading assessment

Think back over the poetry you have read in this chapter and remind yourself of the reading skills you have developed. Remember the terminology you have learned and how each poet has used each feature to create particular effects. Now you can demonstrate your skills as you complete this reading assessment.

Read the poem below and answer the questions opposite. The poet, Carol Ann Duffy, writes about the experience of a parent looking at their child sleeping.

'A Child's Sleep' by Carol Ann Duffy
98 words

I stood at the edge of my child's sleep
hearing her breathe;
although I could not enter there,
I could not leave.

Line 5
Her sleep was a small wood,
perfumed with flowers;
dark, peaceful, sacred,
acred in hours.

And she was the spirit that lives
Line 10
in the heart of such woods;
without time, without history,
wordlessly good.

I spoke her name, a pebble dropped
in the still night,
Line 15
and saw her stir, both open palms
cupping their soft light;

then went to the window. The greater dark
outside the room
gazed back, maternal, wise,
Line 20
with its face of moon.

Unit 5: Reading assessment

Answer the following questions.

1 Choose three quotations from the first stanza to support these statements about the relationships in the poem. Choose one quotation for each statement.

- The speaker feels separate from the child.
- The speaker feels fascinated by watching the sleeping child.
- The poet uses contrast to show the separation of parent and child.

2 Read stanzas 2 and 3. The poet uses two extended metaphors.

a. What does the first metaphor compare sleep to? Explain what this metaphor suggests about the child's sleep.

b. What does the second metaphor compare the child to? Explain what this metaphor suggests about the child.

3 Look carefully at the final stanza of the poem. Explain how you think the ending links to the beginning of the poem. Use quotations to support your explanation.

> **Tip** ✓
>
> Think about who is watching and who is being watched.

4 Having read this poem, a student said:

> *In this poem the poet uses language to create a peaceful and thoughtful mood.*

Do you agree? Use evidence from the poem to support your answer. You might consider:

- the setting and relationships presented
- the poetic voice
- rhyme
- rhythm
- repetition.

95

4 Autobiography and reflection

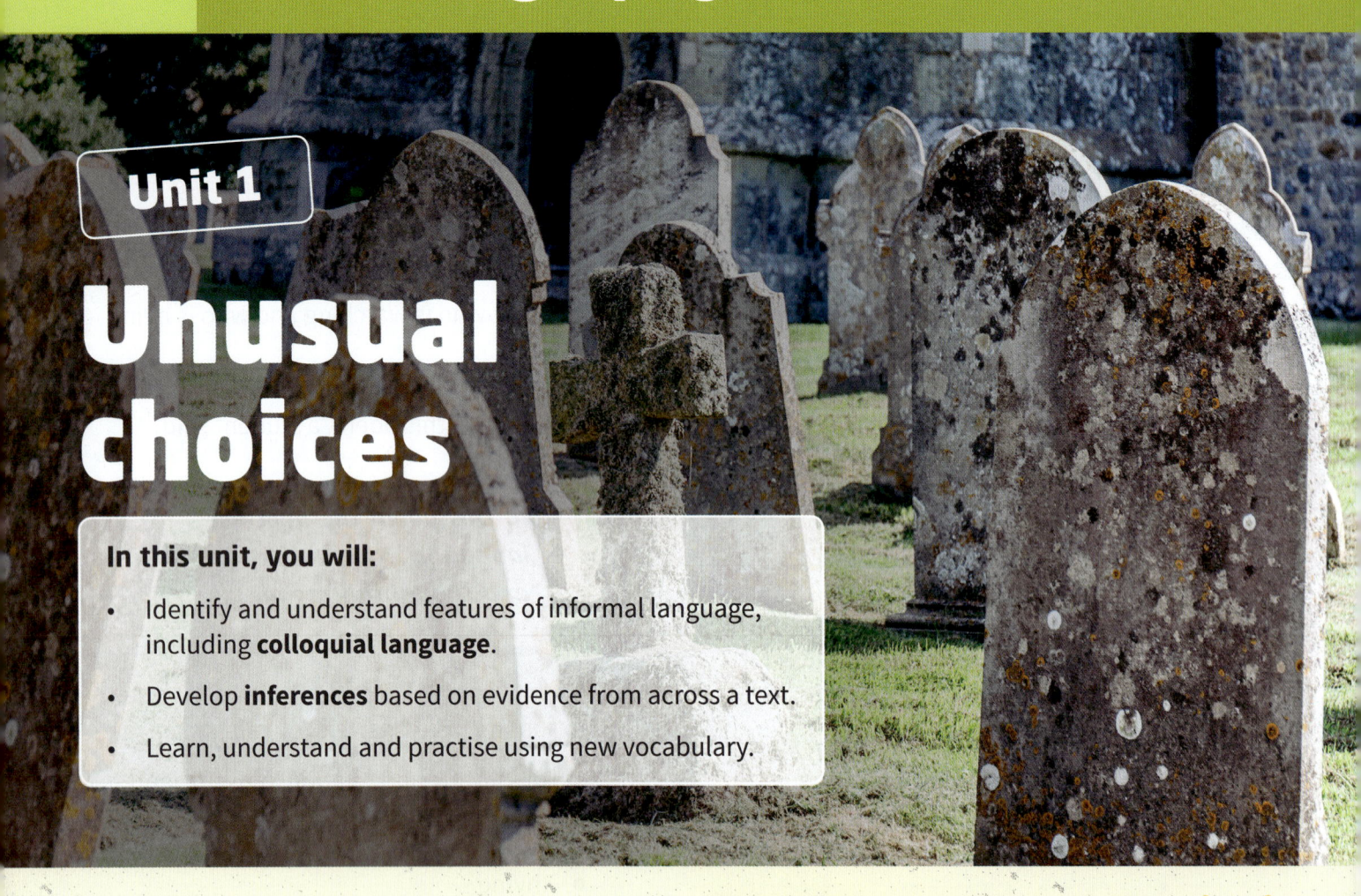

Unit 1

Unusual choices

In this unit, you will:

- Identify and understand features of informal language, including **colloquial language**.
- Develop **inferences** based on evidence from across a text.
- Learn, understand and practise using new vocabulary.

The writer of an **autobiography** writes about their own life. The writer of a **biography** writes about someone else's life. Reading about other people's lives can help you reflect on *your* own life and consider your future. It can also help you to forget about yourself for a while and understand more about different experiences and views.

The extract on page 97 is taken from a book that records the lives of people in an English village from the late 1800s to the 1960s. This book was written after the writer talked to people about their lives. He used the words of these interviews to create a record of their lives.

Key terms

autobiography the story of a person's life, written by that person

biography the story of a person's life, written by someone else

colloquial language the informal, spoken language we use every day in social situations; not suitable for formal speech or writing

inference a sensible suggestion of what is meant, based on clues given in the text

Ready, set, go!

As you read the extract opposite, think about the kind of man you picture in your mind speaking these words.

Unit 1: Unusual choices

Extract from *Akenfield* by Ronald Blythe
465 words

William Russ, aged sixty-one, gravedigger

I started digging graves when I was twelve years old and before I left school. I began by helping an old man and by the time I was thirteen I could do the job as well as I can now. I dug graves before my voice broke – there now! People would look down into the hole and see a child. The work didn't upset me; I took it in my stride. Right from a little boy – if Mother was alive she'd be able to tell you – I used to bury guinea-pigs, rabbits, all sorts of things. I had about fifty rabbits and when one died I would make a coffin for it, get my choir **surplice** from the church **vestry** and read the Burial Service over it. So burying has been in my blood from a child. I never wanted to do anything else; graves are my vocation.

I've been at the church, official-like, since 1918. I was employed when I was thirteen and I've buried damn-near the whole of the old village, every one of them. I remember the first grave I dug. It was for a man named Hayman. I've got all my burials down since the day I started, men, women and children.

So far as funerals are concerned, we've gone from one extreme to the other. Bodies used to be kept in the house for twelve days. Everyone kept the body at home for as long as they could then; they didn't care to part with it, you see. Now they can't get it out quick enough. They didn't like hurrying about anything when I was young, particularly about death. They were afraid that the **corpse** might still be alive – that was the real reason for hanging on to it. People have a **post-mortem** now and it's all settled in a minute, but there's no doubt that years ago there were a rare lot of folk who got buried alive. When a sick man passed on the doctor was told, but he never came to look at the corpse. He just wrote out the death certificate.

There was an old man near Framlingham, old Micah Hibble, he was laid out dead three times. The last time he was actually in his coffin and waiting for the funeral to begin. When I asked, 'Any more for a last look before he's screwed down?' there was the usual nuisance pushing his way through the mourners and saying, 'Yes, I do!' Trust somebody to get you fiddling about and making the funeral late. The bell was going, so you know how late it was. Anyway, when this man looked in the coffin he saw that Micah had moved. Well do you know, he recovered!

---

surplice – loose white ceremonial robe worn by clergy and choristers at Christian church services
vestry – a room in a church where the clergy and choir put ceremonial robes on
corpse – dead body
post-mortem – a medical examination after death to confirm the reason for death

4.1 Chapter 4: Autobiography and reflection

⚡ Word power

Re-read the extract on page 97. Pay particular attention to the target words and **phrases** listed below. As you read, think about what each of the target words or phrases might mean in context.

Your target words and phrases for this section are:

- voice broke
- took it in my stride
- in my blood
- vocation
- recovered

These target words and phrases have been highlighted in blue in the extract on page 97.

> **Key terms**
>
> **figuratively** used imaginatively to convey an idea, often in the form of a comparison
>
> **literally** used exactly as stated, with the most obvious meaning
>
> **phrase** a group of words that forms a unit

1 William Russ describes digging graves as his vocation.

  a. Use the Target word list on pages 174–175 to check the meaning of the word 'vocation'. Then choose the best explanation for its use in the extract.

  - He drifted into the job by chance.
  - He was made to work at digging graves.
  - It was a natural choice of job for him.

  b. Look how the word 'vocation' is included in the sentence below.

  > *Formula One was a vocation for Lewis Hamilton. What started as a hobby in kart racing became the basis for his job.*

  Write your own sentence about a celebrity or someone you know, using the word 'vocation'.

2 Look up the word 'recovered' in the Target word list on pages 174–175. Two definitions are given. Which definition best fits the gravedigger's use of this word to describe old Micah Hibble?

Do you feel that you have a vocation?

Unit 1: Unusual choices

3 The underlined words in the phrases below are used **figuratively** rather than **literally**.

Read each phrase and its literal meaning. Write an explanation of the figurative meaning of each phrase. The first one has been done for you.

Phrase	Literal meaning	Figurative meaning
my voice broke	my voice stopped working	my voice got deeper as part of adolescence
I took it in my stride	I collected something while I was walking	
burying has been in my blood from a child	burying has been running through the veins in my body	

4 What impression do the phrases in the table give about the speaker and his life? Choose one of the options below for each phrase.

'I dug graves before my voice broke'

'The work didn't upset me; I took it in my stride.'

'So burying has been in my blood from a child.'

He was a) old / b) a teenager / c) a child / d) an adult when he started working.

He had a a) lazy / b) calm / c) anxious / d) energetic attitude to his work.

He had always been a) frightened of / b) made to watch / c) naturally interested in burials.

Knowledge and understanding

Look back at the extract on page 97 and answer the following questions.

1 When did the man begin the job of digging graves?

2 What activities did the gravedigger do as a child that suggest this was the ideal job for him?

3 What does the gravedigger say in paragraph 2 that tells us he is now an old man?

4 How has the gravedigger's experience of burying people changed since he first started his job? You will need to make inferences from what you read in the text.

99

4.1 Chapter 4: Autobiography and reflection

📖 Reading skills

The writer of this text has recorded the informal spoken words of an old gravedigger. The words reveal his character and his attitude towards his work.

Look at the language features in the Key terms panel on the right. Some of them are identified in the notes around the next extract.

figurative language — *exclamation and filler*

'I dug graves **before my voice broke** – **there now!** People would look down into the hole and see a child. The work didn't upset me; **I took it in my stride**. Right from a little boy – if Mother was alive she'd be able to tell you – I used to bury **guinea-pigs, rabbits,** all sorts of things. I had about fifty rabbits and when one died I would make a coffin for it, get my choir **surplice** from the church **vestry** and read the **Burial Service** over it. So burying has **been in my blood** from a child.'

— *specific details*
— *specialist terms*

Key terms

exclamation a remark expressing surprise or excitement

figurative language words or expressions with a meaning that is different from the literal meaning

filler meaningless words, phrases or sounds that mark a hesitation in speech, e.g. *uh, you know*

slang informal words and phrases usually found in speech rather than writing

specialist term word or phrase that shows specific knowledge about a topic

specific detail small bit of information

---

1 Now read the two extracts below, identifying as many of the language features listed in the Key terms panel as you can. Copy and complete a table like the one started on the right.

'I've been at the church, official-like, since 1918. I was employed when I was thirteen and I've buried damn-near the whole of the old village, every one of them. I remember the first grave I dug. It was for a man named Hayman. I've got all my burials down since the day I started, men, women and children.'

'So far as funerals are concerned, we've gone from one extreme to the other. Bodies used to be kept in the house for twelve days. Everyone kept the body at home for as long as they could then; they didn't care to part with it, you see. Now they can't get it out quick enough.'

Language	Example from the extract
Slang	'official-like' 'you see'
Figurative language	
	'I remember the first grave I dug...'
Exclamation	
Specific details	
Specialist terms	

100

Unit 1: Unusual choices

2 Now look at what some of these features convey about people's attitudes towards death. Read each extract below and complete the sentence to explain its effect.

a.

'The work didn't upset me; I took it in my stride.'

The gravedigger's use of figurative language emphasises…

'they didn't care to part with it, you see.'

The gravedigger's use of the filler…

How would you feel in this situation?

! Check your skills

Write a paragraph explaining the changes William Russ has noticed in the way people approach death and funerals since when he was a boy. Comment on how his language choices help to convey his feelings about this.

Support your points with references to the extract, using the correct terms to identify language features.

101

4.2 Chapter 4: Autobiography and reflection

Unit 2
Early goals

In this unit, you will:
- Understand how a writer organises a text using paragraphs.
- Understand how information in a text can be presented in **chronological order** using **adverbs** and **adverbials of time**.
- Learn, understand and practise using new vocabulary.

Biographers research information about the life of a particular person to help them to write an account of that life. They must think about what their reader will find interesting and in what order they should present the information.

The text on page 103 is from a biography of Lord Alan Sugar, the entrepreneur and presenter of the TV show, *The Apprentice*. In this extract the biographer, Charlie Burden, gives information about the young Sugar's early experiences of work and earning money to show how his early habits led to his later success.

Key terms

biographer an author who writes about the life of another person

chronological order the order in which actions or events actually happen

adverb a word that gives more information about a verb, an adjective or another adverb

adverbial of time adverbials that say how when something is taking place e.g. tomorrow or later

Ready, set, go!

As you read, think about Lord Sugar's early experiences of work. What do they show about his character?

Unit 2: Early goals

Lord Sugar by Charlie Burden
453 words

It was in the streets of East London, in the early hours of the morning, that Sugar first showed his **work ethic**. As a child he earned his first wages by wandering around the estate, knocking on people's doors and asking if they had any fizzy drink bottles he could **redeem** at the local shop. A small fee was available to anyone who returned the bottles to the shop and he was amazed that everyone was not automatically taking them back to claim their **deposit**.

[…]

He had got the taste of pocketing cash and it was through a not unrelated, if more ambitious, route that he arrived at his next money-making scheme. At 13 years of age he was given a present that would refresh more than his thirst. In those days, a ginger beer plant was popular in many British households. Thought to have originated from the **Royal Botanic Gardens** in Kew, this was not a plant in the sense of a green stem with leaves or flowers. Instead, the ginger beer plant was a sloppy white mass, **comprising** bacteria, yeast and fungus. This would be kept in a jar by excited Brits and topped up daily with teaspoons of ginger and sugar, together with lemon juice and water. The substance would then produce a bubbly liquid to be **siphoned** out of the jar and put into bottles.

Sugar soon had his own ginger beer to sell and was ready to take on the soft drink giants of the world – or at least in his immediate surroundings. He would sell his home-brewed (or home-fermented, to be precise) ginger beer to his fellow kids on the estate. **Undercutting** the likes of Coca-Cola, he proved a popular **merchant** and was soon bringing in a semi-decent income. His **entrepreneurial streak** was increasing as he sought more and more ways to pocket cash. More famously, he also worked with a local greengrocer. He would rise in the early hours of Saturday morning to boil beetroot for the man, again earning himself some much-welcomed spending money.

'It wasn't a case of deciding to do that,' he says of this unglamorous Saturday job. 'It was quite common for people who lived in my council block to have a Saturday job, a holiday job, a paper round or whatever. It was necessary – if you wanted your own pocket money you had to go and get it yourself.' He took whatever jobs were on offer. When one opportunity disappeared or was outshone by something better, he simply moved on. Some were more exciting than others, but whatever the challenge and opportunity was, he was happy to take it and to approach it with his sense of focus, determination and effort.

---

work ethic – attitude to work
redeem – get back
deposit – money paid as a guarantee (in this case to return the bottle)
Royal Botanic Gardens – famous gardens in London
comprising – made up of
siphoned – drawn through a tube
undercutting – selling at a lower price
merchant – person involved in trade
entrepreneurial streak – ability to set up a business to make money

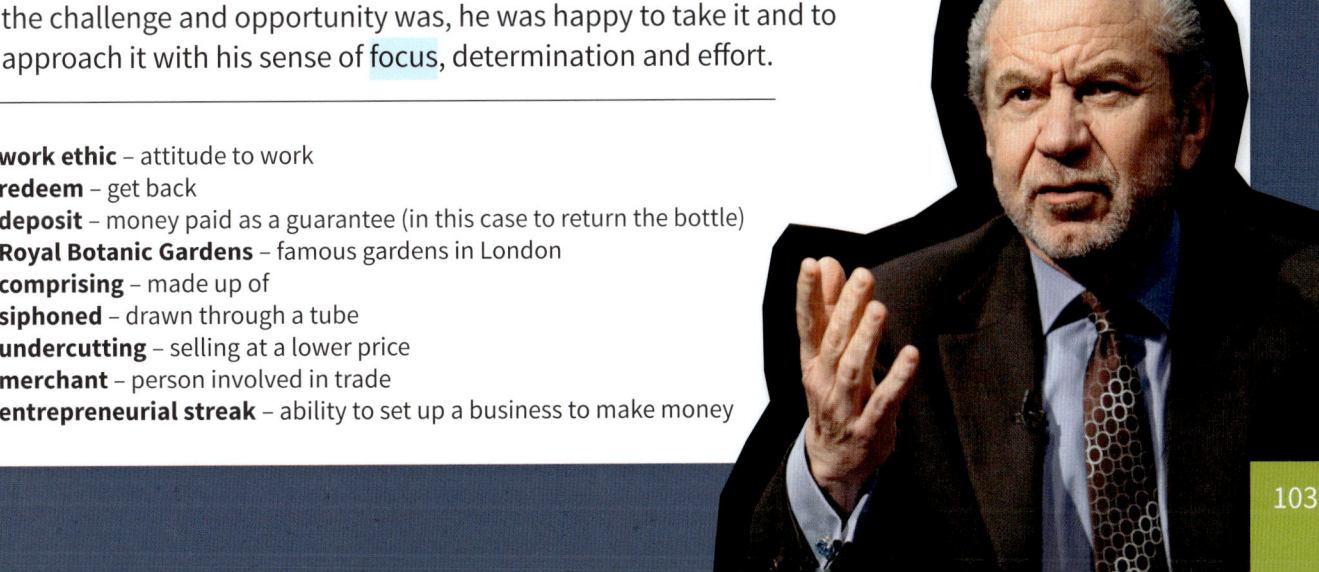

4.2 Chapter 4: Autobiography and reflection

⚡ Word power

Re-read the extract on page 103. Pay attention to the target words listed below. As you read, think about what each of these words might mean in context.

Your target words for this section are:

- ambitious
- originated
- opportunity
- focus

These target words have been highlighted in blue in the extract on page 103.

1 The word 'ambitious' has two meanings:
- it describes a person who has a lot of ambition to succeed
- it describes a plan or idea that is difficult and demanding.

In the extract, we are told that Sugar's second money-making scheme was more 'ambitious' than his first. Which is the correct meaning of the word in this context? Explain your answer carefully.

2 Look up the word 'originated' in the Target word list on pages 174–175.

This is how the word is used in the extract:

> Thought to have originated from the Royal Botanic Gardens in Kew

Rewrite the sentence below without using the word 'originated':

> *Most people thought that the plant...*

Unit 2: Early goals

3 An 'opportunity' is a suitable or convenient time for doing something. Write a sentence using the word 'opportunity'. It could be about Sugar and his attitude to earning money, or it could be about yourself. You could use one of the following sentence starters:

When he saw an...

If I have the...

4 The biographer talks about Sugar's 'sense of focus, determination and effort'. What does the word 'focus' suggest about the young Sugar? Choose the correct explanation.

- He had good eye-sight.
- He concentrated on his goal.
- He had a good sense of humour.

Knowledge and understanding

Look back at the extract on page 103 and answer the following questions.

1 Why did Sugar ask people if they had any fizzy drink bottles?

2 In the second paragraph, we are told that Sugar was given 'a present that would refresh more than his thirst'.

   a. What was this present?

   b. What did it refresh, other than his thirst? (Think about what else the present motivated Sugar to do.)

3 What did Sugar have to give the plant in order for it to produce ginger beer?

4 When Sugar found that an opportunity to make money disappeared, what did he do?

4.2 Chapter 4: Autobiography and reflection

✏️ Writing skills

1 The biographer uses paragraphs to give his writing a **structure**. Write a brief **summary** of each paragraph using the grid below. The first one is done for you.

> **Tip**
>
> Remember that a paragraph can mark a new topic, place, time or speaker.

Paragraph	Topic
1	*Sugar's first money-making scheme was to collect and return empty drink bottles*
2	
3	
4	

2 The extract uses adverbs and adverbials of time to link events, telling the reader *when* things happened. For example,

> Sugar **first** showed his work ethic…

Link each of the adverbs and adverbials of time below to the event it is used with in the extract on page 103.

> **Key terms**
>
> **structure** how a text is ordered, the connections made between ideas and topics, and where the writer is directing the reader's focus
>
> **summary** a short text giving just the main points

Adverbs and adverbials of time

- In those days
- At 13 years of age
- As a child
- as he sought
- Sugar soon

Unit 2: Early goals

3 List the events in chronological order. Refer back to the text to help you.

Events

a. he earned his first wages

b. he was given a present

c. a ginger beer plant was popular

d. had his own ginger beer to sell

e. more and more ways to pocket cash

4 Plan your own account about a time when you, or someone you know, did something for the first time, for example trying out a new sport, visiting a place for the first time or making something new.

- Identify four or five chronological points in time that can order your account.
- You might like to tell the account to your partner using the plan you have made to help you remember the structure. The following adverbs and adverbials of time may also be helpful:

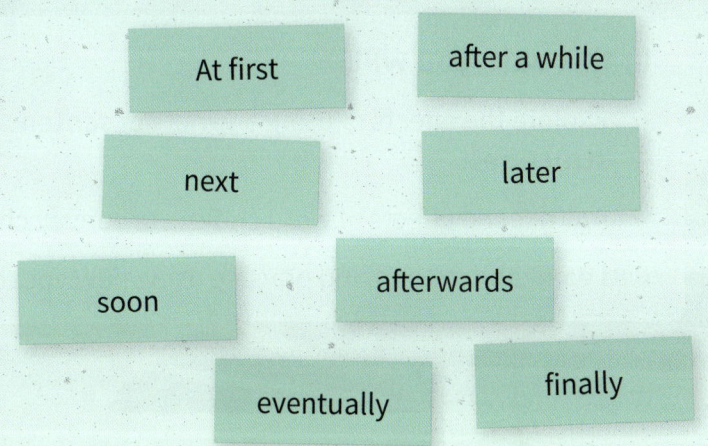

At first

after a while

next

later

soon

afterwards

eventually

finally

! Check your skills

Write a full account about a time when you, or someone you know, did something you found difficult or challenging, such as joining a new club or going away without parents. If you wish, use the plan you created in Activity 4.

- Choose a focus for each paragraph.
- Use adverbs and adverbials of time to help your reader understand when events happened.
- Organise your narrative in chronological order.
- If possible, use at least one of the target words in your writing.

When you have finished your writing, check your work for any errors in grammar, spelling or punctuation.

4.3 Chapter 4: Autobiography and reflection

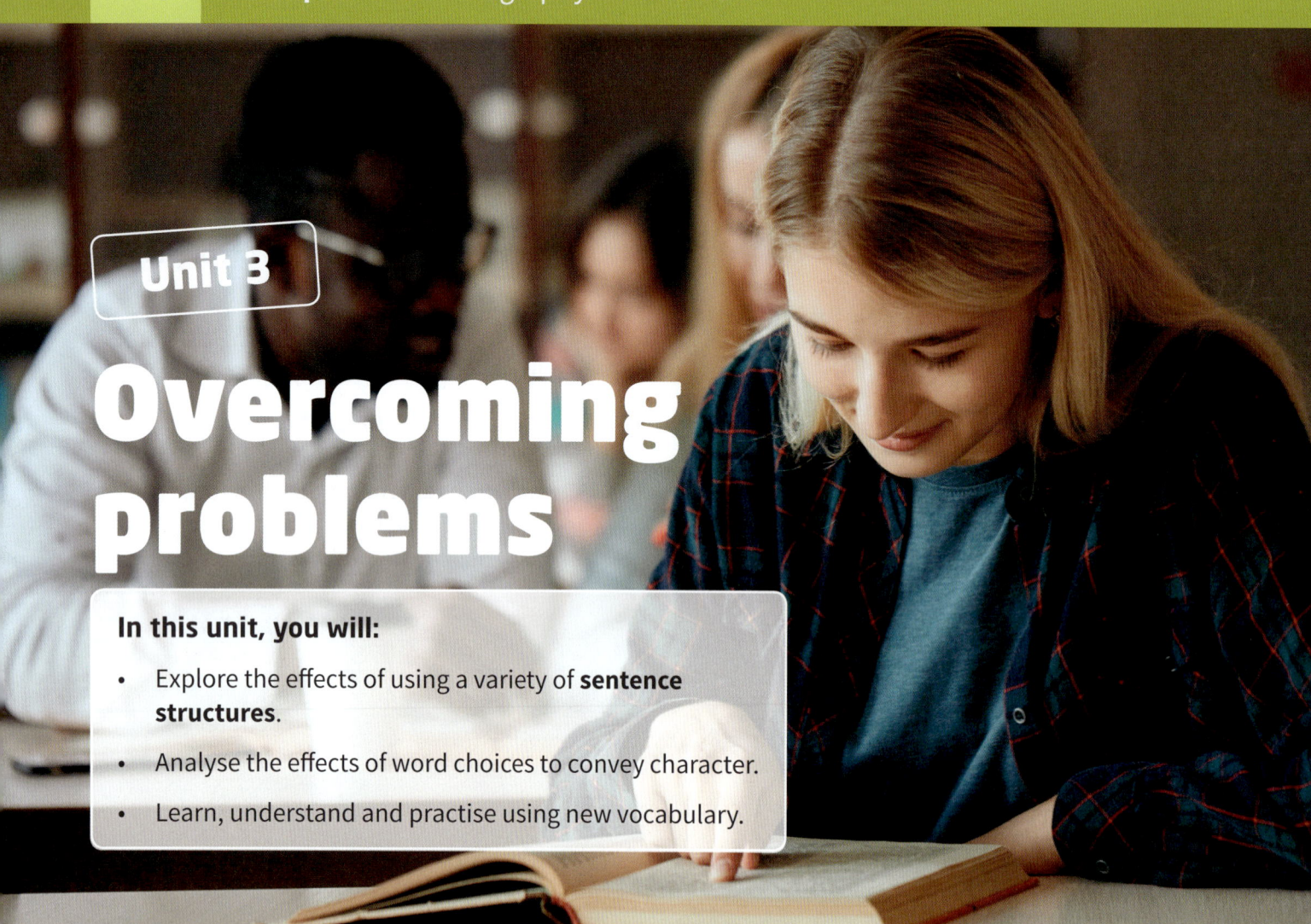

Unit 3

Overcoming problems

In this unit, you will:

- Explore the effects of using a variety of **sentence structures**.
- Analyse the effects of word choices to convey character.
- Learn, understand and practise using new vocabulary.

The extract on page 109 comes from a collection of autobiographical writing that tells how various high achievers overcame challenges in life. Here, ballerina Darcey Bussell shows how she faced some challenges in her life and used them as a strength.

Key term

sentence structure how a sentence is put together, including word and punctuation choices and word order

Ready, set, go!

As you read the extract opposite, look for phrases that suggest that Darcey Bussell is a strong and determined person.

Unit 3: Overcoming problems

Extract about Darcey Bussell CBE from *Creative Successful Dyslexic* by Margaret Rooke
462 words

The **diagnosis** of **dyslexia** didn't come until secondary school at 11. When I was told, I felt I would have been better off not knowing. My mother had always made me believe that if I really wanted to achieve I could do it just with hard work, so I always thought I would improve. The **terminology** confirmed that my differences were part of me and the diagnosis lay heavily on my shoulders.

I went to extra classes for people with dyslexia at St Bartholomew's Hospital. Here I found out that I was turning words around the wrong way as I read them and wrote them. When I understood this I could help myself correct them. [...]

I realised that whole pages of words overwhelmed me and I was taught to put a piece of card over the rest of the page while I read a line, which was a big help.

At school, which was a stage school, I had to memorise poems and I managed this. I had learned by now that if I wanted something enough I had to believe it was possible and fight to achieve it. I remember one teacher saying to me that I had the right physique to be a decent dancer and I thought, 'That's it.' It was my perfect outlet and I was determined to achieve this. [...]

When I was 13, I passed a three-day **audition** to get accepted into the Royal Ballet School but my skills were far behind the others. In my first year the older girls would look through a window laughing at me while I tried to copy the ballet steps of the others. I even burst into tears after my first disastrous first-year exams. It did seem to take me longer to learn in those early days – but **adversity** does drive me forward. A year later I suddenly made an improvement in my dance. I had developed a real hunger to succeed and an obsession with being a ballerina. It was like the door to my future had opened.

I was still having problems with my GCSEs. I always thought the clever children at school weren't doing any work but of course they were. As soon as I realised this, it occurred to me that all I needed to do was put in extra hours. Then I could keep up. This gave me a new work ethic, which really helped.

One GCSE I desperately wanted to do was History of Ballet. I was told not to go in for it as I wouldn't pass but I thought, 'You can't say that.' Being as stubborn as I was, I took the exam and passed it anyway. Again I had shown myself I could achieve; things could happen for me.

---

diagnosis – a decision made by a specialist about a medical or other condition
dyslexia – a common type of learning difficulty that can cause problems with reading, writing and spelling
terminology – technical description
audition – a trial performance, by a dancer, actor or musician to judge the standard of their talent
adversity – hardship or misfortune

Darcey Bussell is now a judge on the TV show Strictly Come Dancing.

4.3 Chapter 4: Autobiography and reflection

⚡ Word power

Re-read the extract on page 109. Pay particular attention to the target words and phrases listed below. As you read, think about what each of the words might mean in the extract.

Your target words and phrases for this section are:

- achieve
- overwhelmed
- work ethic
- stubborn

These target words and phrases have been highlighted in blue in the extract on page 109.

She studied really hard so that she would achieve good grades in her exams.

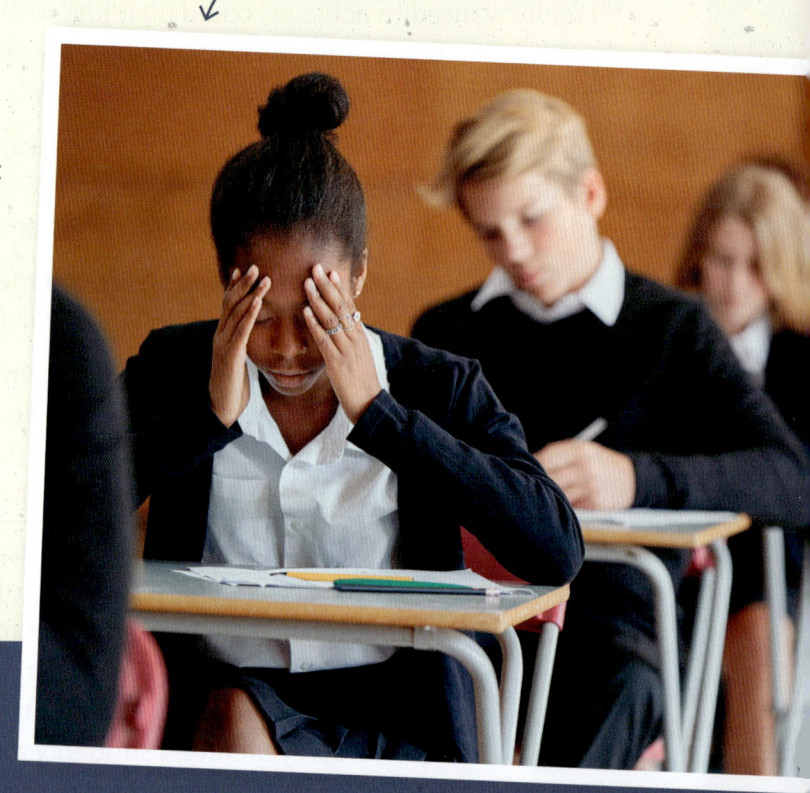

1 Which of the words or phrases below are closest in meaning to the target words as used in the extract? Give a reason for each choice.

a. 'if I really wanted to achieve'

finish   succeed   gain

b. 'whole pages of words overwhelmed me'

exhausted   thrilled   were too much for

110

Unit 3: Overcoming problems

2   **a.** Look up the word 'stubborn' in the Target word list on pages 174–175. Three definitions are given. Which meaning is the right one in the extract below?

> 'Being as stubborn as I was, I took the exam and passed it anyway.'

     b. Think about someone you know who can be stubborn at times. Write a sentence about them, using the word 'stubborn' with an example of when they show this attitude.

3   The expression 'work ethic' describes the attitude and values someone displays towards their work.

> 'This gave me a new work ethic, which really helped.'

     a. Explain what Bussell did to develop a new work ethic.

     b. Now write your own sentence about someone who has a good work ethic. Explain what they do to show a good work ethic.

4   Now it's your turn to use some of the target words in your own writing. Write a paragraph explaining an aspect of your life where you have overcome a difficulty or are making progress in doing this. This might be in sport, school life, friendships or life at home.

Include at least two of the target words. You could use the following sentence starter or begin using your own words.

> *Everyone has difficulties to face in their life. For me, …*

Knowledge and understanding

1   How old was Bussell when she realised she had dyslexia?

2   Why did she feel it might have been better if she had not had the diagnosis?

3   Explain a method that Bussell used to help improve her reading and writing skills.

4   This autobiography explains various difficulties that Bussell had to overcome in her early life. List four challenges that she faced.

5   What did Bussell realise when she was doing her GCSEs?

4.3 Chapter 4: Autobiography and reflection

📖 Reading skills

A well-written text to inform and engage readers, like the one on page 109, contains a range of sentence structures. A skilled writer is likely to use a mix of long and short sentences, including **single** and **multi-clause sentences**.

Some multi-clause sentences are fairly long. Some single-clause sentences are quite short. The different lengths can have particular impact. For example, a long multi-clause sentence might use additional clauses to build up lots of information. A short sentence might be used to create impact or to draw attention to an important point.

Look at the extracts and notes below. The notes show the different sentence structures that Bussell uses and the effects they create.

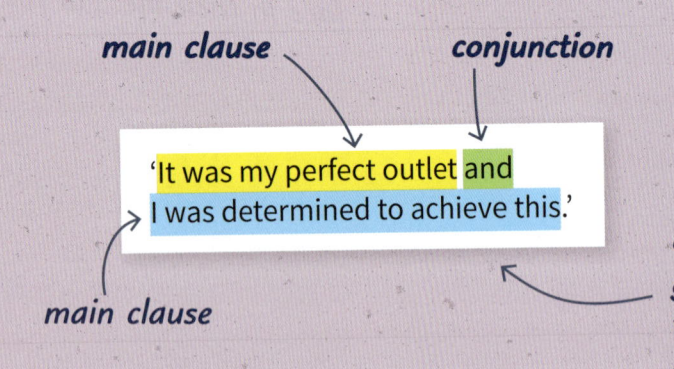

main clause → 'It was my perfect outlet *and* — *conjunction*

main clause → I was determined to achieve this.'

→ *a long multi-clause sentence giving information by joining two ideas — the outlet of dance and her determination*

'I even burst into tears after my first disastrous first-year exams.'

a short single-clause sentence emphasising the harsh effect of Bussell's difficulties

> **Key terms**
>
> **conjunction** a linking word that joins words or groups of words together, e.g. *if, but, and*
>
> **main clause** a clause that contains a subject and a verb, and makes sense on its own
>
> **multi-clause sentence** a sentence made up of more than one clause, each with its own verb
>
> **single-clause sentence** (also known as a simple sentence) a sentence with one main clause

Unit 3: Overcoming problems

1 Now look at the sentences below. Identify whether each is a single or a multi-clause sentence, and write a comment on the effect they create for the reader.

> 'It did seem to take me longer to learn in those early days – but adversity does drive me forward.'

> 'I was still having problems with my GCSEs.'

> 'I always thought the clever children at school weren't doing any work but of course they were.'

> 'Then I could keep up.'

2 a. Bussell uses a variety of word choices to explain her reactions to her situation and actions. Identify a powerful word in each sentence below and explain what it suggests about her character.

> 'I had learned by now that if I wanted something enough I had to believe it was possible and fight to achieve it.'

> 'It did seem to take me longer to learn in those early days – but adversity does drive me forward.'

> 'It was my perfect outlet and I was determined to achieve it.'

b. Find another powerful word that Bussell uses in the extract and comment on what it suggests about her character.

! Check your skills

Write two paragraphs to explain how this autobiography conveys the character of Darcey Bussell. What does it suggest about her as a person? How does it suggest this?

You might consider how she uses:
- information about the difficulties she faced
- a variety of sentence structures for effect
- powerful word choices to emphasise her strength of character.

Read back over your writing to check it.
- Does it all make sense?
- Have you used quotations to prove your points?
- Have you commented on their effects?

113

4.4 Chapter 4: Autobiography and reflection

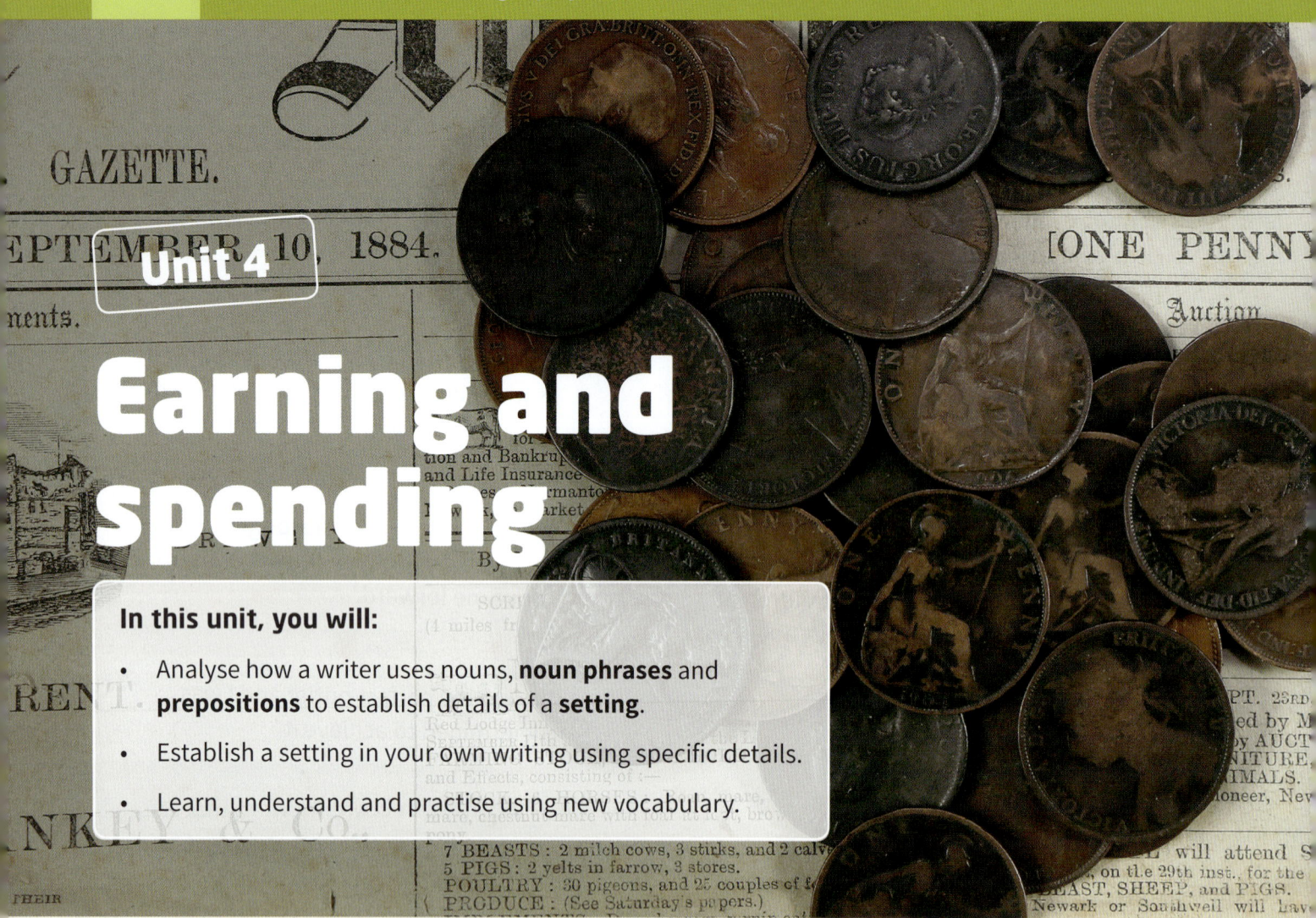

Unit 4
Earning and spending

In this unit, you will:

- Analyse how a writer uses nouns, **noun phrases** and **prepositions** to establish details of a **setting**.
- Establish a setting in your own writing using specific details.
- Learn, understand and practise using new vocabulary.

A writer's description of a place can be important. Settings help us to understand more about characters and engage us in imagining the events of a story. In autobiographical texts, precise details of setting help convey a sense of truth and reality. In 19th-century texts, setting can be crucial in helping us learn about lives and experiences that were very different from our own.

The extract on page 115 comes from autobiographical writing by Charles Dickens. When he was 12 years old, he started working ten-hour days at Warren's Blacking Warehouse in London. He earned six shillings a week pasting labels on jars of shoe polish. This money helped to support his family. In this extract, he describes his workplace, his work and his memories of the food he could buy with his earnings.

Key terms

noun phrase a group of words that has a noun as its head or key word. All the words in the group tell us more about the head noun, e.g. *a big muddy puddle* ('puddle' is the head noun)

preposition a word used with a noun to show place, position or time, e.g. *behind, before, up, on*

setting the time and place where the action of a story happens

Ready, set, go!

As you read the extract opposite, try to picture this workplace in your mind. How would it feel to arrive here for work?

114

Unit 4: Earning and spending

Extract from Autobiographical writing by Charles Dickens
427 words

The **blacking-warehouse** was the last house on the left-hand side of the way, at old Hungerford Stairs. It was a crazy, tumble-down old house, **abutting** of course on the river, and literally overrun with rats. Its **wainscoted** rooms and its rotten floors and staircase, and the old grey rats swarming down in the cellars, and the sound of their squeaking and scuffling coming up the stairs at all times, and the dirt and decay of the place, rise up visibly before me, as if I were there again. The **counting-house** was on the first floor, looking over the **coal-barges** and the river. There was a recess in it, in which I was to sit and work. My work was to cover the pots of **paste-blacking**; first with a piece of oil-paper, and then with a piece of blue paper; to tie them round with a string; and then to clip the paper close and neat, all round, until it looked as smart as a pot of ointment from an **apothecary**'s shop. When a certain number of **grosses** of pots had attained this pitch of perfection, I was to paste on each a printed label, and then go on again with more pots. […]

Dickens' pots had to look as smart as this old pot for ointment.

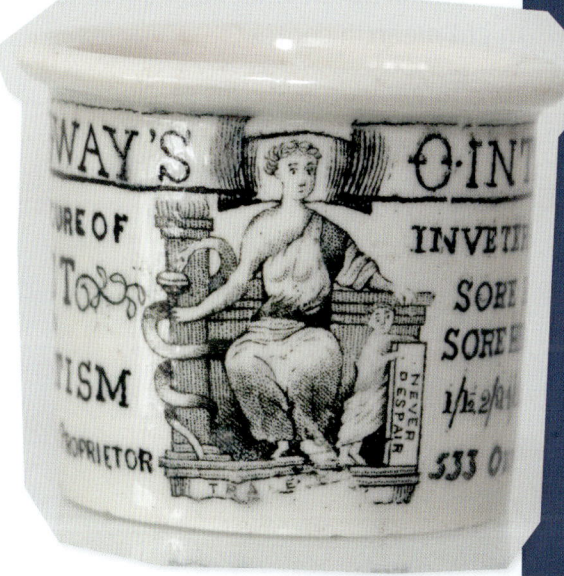

[…] in going to Hungerford Stairs of a morning, I could not resist the stale pastry put out at half-price on trays at the **confectioners**' doors in Tottenham Court Road; and I often spent in that, the money I should have kept for my dinner. Then I went without my dinner, or bought a roll, or a slice of **pudding**. There were two pudding shops between which I was divided, according to my finances. One was in a court close to St Martin's Church (at the back of the church) which is now removed altogether. The pudding at that shop was made with currants, and was rather a special pudding, but was dear: two penn'orth not being larger than a penn'orth of more ordinary pudding. A good shop for the latter was in the Strand. It was a stout, **hale** pudding, heavy, and flabby; with great raisins in it, stuck in whole, at great distances apart. It came up hot, at about noon every day; and many and many a day did I dine off it.

We had half-an-hour I think, for tea. When I had money enough, I used to go to a coffee-shop and have half-a-pint of coffee, and a slice of bread and butter. When I had no money, I took a turn in Covent Garden Market, and stared at the pineapples.

---

blacking-warehouse – large building where black shoe polish was stored
abutting – next to, joining
wainscoted – panelled with wood
counting-house – office
coal-barges – boats carrying coal

paste-blacking – a type of polish
apothecary – chemist
grosses – groups of 144 (12 dozen)
confectioners – bakers
pudding – cake or bun
hale – hearty and substantial

115

4.4 Chapter 4: Autobiography and reflection

⚡ Word power

Re-read the extract on page 115. Pay particular attention to the target words listed below. As you read, think about what each of the target words might mean in context.

Your target words for this section are:

- swarming
- decay
- visibly
- recess
- stout

These target words have been highlighted in blue in the extract on page 115.

What do rats do that might be described as swarming?

1 Dickens uses the word 'swarming' to describe the rats.

　a. What impression does this word give you about the rats? If you need to, check the meaning in the Target word list on pages 174–175.

　b. In the sentence below, find another similar word that adds to the idea of the building 'swarming' with rats.

> 'It was a crazy, tumble-down old house, abutting of course on the river, and literally overrun with rats.'

2 Dickens' choice of the word 'decay' conveys the strength of his memory of this rotting setting. Write down three other words that 'decay' suggests to you about this building.

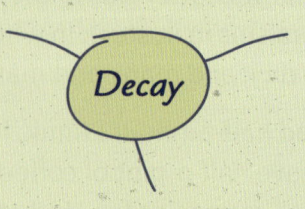

Decay

3 The noun 'recess' means a small space created by building part of a wall further back from the rest of the wall. A recess is often used in a room to tuck in shelves or a table. Look back to where this word is used in the extract. What impression does this give about Dickens' working space?

Unit 4: Earning and spending

4 Find the word 'visibly' in the extract and consider its meaning. Make an informed guess by thinking about other related words, such as:

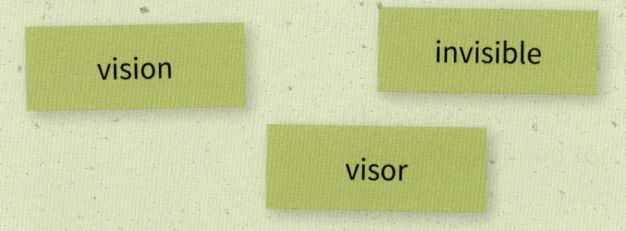

- vision
- invisible
- visor

Write out your definition of the word 'visibly' in the context of this extract. Check the Target word list on pages 174–175 to check if you guessed correctly.

5 Look at the following sentence from the extract

> 'It was a stout, hale pudding, heavy, and flabby'

What other words with a similar meaning to 'stout' could replace it in this sentence? (Check its meaning in the Target word list if necessary.)

6 Now choose two target words and include them in a sentence of your own, perhaps describing a place you know well.

Knowledge and understanding

1 Pick out three details from the first paragraph of the extract that suggest the young Dickens' working environment was unpleasant.

2 How would you describe the kind of work that Dickens had to do?

- Use quotations and explain the reasons for your answer.
- You might like to choose from the words below to help you.

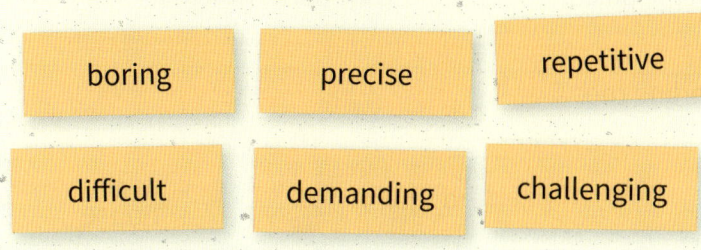

- boring
- precise
- repetitive
- difficult
- demanding
- challenging

3 Dickens tells how he spent his money on food from places near his work. Make a list of the things he bought to eat and drink.

4 Dickens uses noun phrases to give detail about some of the food he remembers. These details help the reader to imagine how this poor boy felt about the pleasure of food. Look at the following noun phrases:

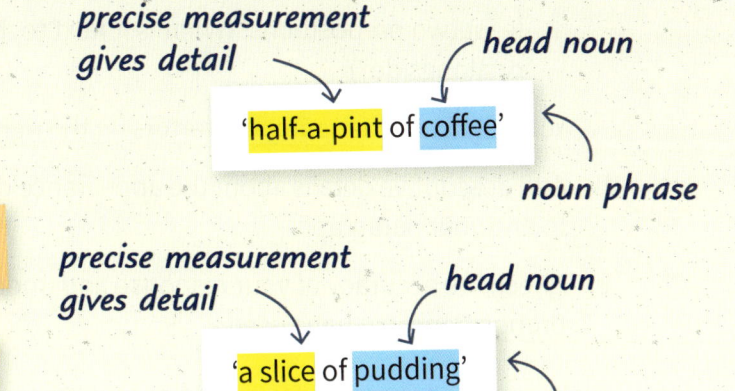

precise measurement gives detail → 'half-a-pint of coffee' ← *head noun* / *noun phrase*

precise measurement gives detail → 'a slice of pudding' ← *head noun* / *noun phrase*

Write down two more noun phrases that Dickens uses. Circle the head (the main noun) and underline the words that add more detail about the noun.

117

4.4 Chapter 4: Autobiography and reflection

✏️ Writing skills

Dickens helps the reader to imagine the setting by locating and describing it precisely. He uses prepositions to help give details. Prepositions are words that show time, place or position and are used with a noun.

1 Look at the prepositions highlighted in the extract below. Pick out the last two prepositions in the paragraph, which have not been highlighted.

> 'The blacking-warehouse was the last house **on the left-hand side** of the way, **at** old Hungerford Stairs. It was a crazy, tumble-down old house, abutting of course **on** the river, and literally overrun with rats. Its wainscoted rooms and its rotten floors and staircase, and the old grey rats swarming **down** in the cellars, and the sound of their squeaking and scuffling coming **up** the stairs at all times, and the dirt and decay of the place, rise **up** visibly **before** me, as if I were there again. The counting-house was on the first floor, looking over the coal-barges and the river.'

2 Dickens uses prepositions to give details of the precise location of his workplace.

a. Write two sentences to describe the exact location of a place near you that you would recommend a teenager to visit.

- Sentence 1: Name the place and explain why they should visit.
- Sentence 2: Describe its exact location, using at least two prepositions. (What is it next to, behind or alongside?)

A place I would recommend teenagers visit is...

You might use the sentence starters on the right.

You will find it...

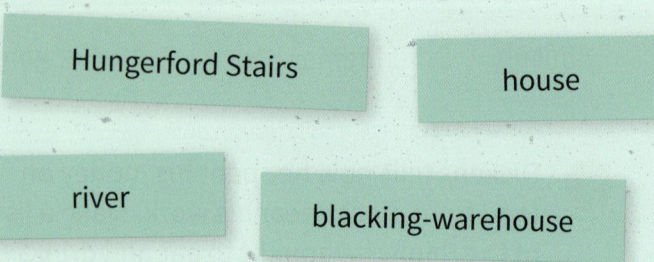

b. Add descriptive details about the appearance of the place, to end your paragraph.

c. Check the accuracy of your response and underline the prepositions you have used.

3 Dickens includes many nouns and noun phrases at the beginning of this extract to help the reader picture where he worked.
Add five more nouns, which Dickens uses in his first paragraph, to this list.

Hungerford Stairs   house   river   blacking-warehouse

Unit 4: Earning and spending

4 Imagine you are Dickens, sitting at his desk in the factory and describing his position and his view. Add three more sentences to the depressing picture Dickens has already created below. Use nouns, noun phrases and prepositions to describe the location precisely.

> 'The counting-house was on the first floor, looking over the coal-barges and the river. There was a recess in it, in which I was to sit and work…'

You might want to use some of the following nouns, noun phrases and prepositions.

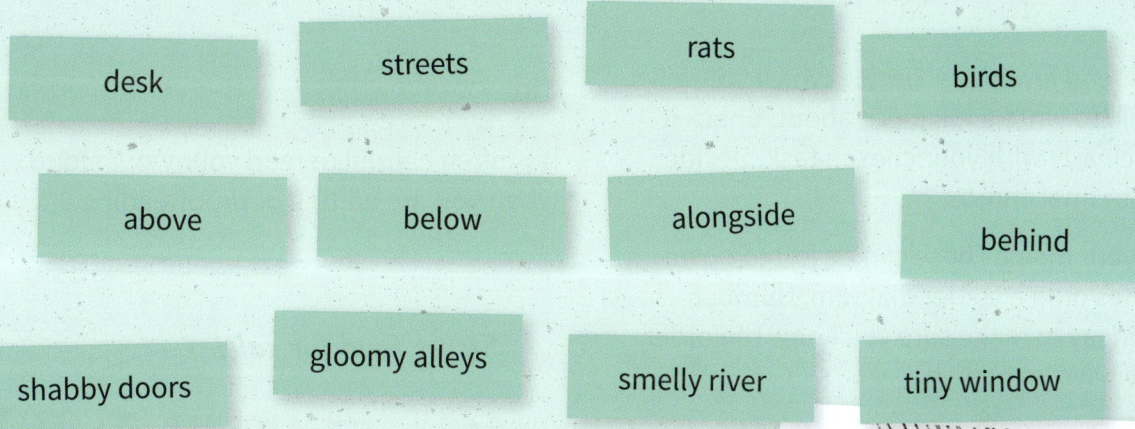

- desk
- streets
- rats
- birds
- above
- below
- alongside
- behind
- shabby doors
- gloomy alleys
- smelly river
- tiny window

! Check your skills

Write at least two paragraphs describing a place, real or imagined, where you do or don't enjoy working. For example, you might think of a particular room at home or school, or in a future workplace.

- Use prepositions to locate it precisely.
- Use nouns and noun phrases to add specific details to build up a picture or your viewpoint.

When you have finished, check your work to ensure it makes sense and there are no grammar, spelling or punctuation mistakes.

The blacking-warehouse was a hard environment for a 12-year-old boy.

4.5 Chapter 4: Autobiography and reflection

Unit 5
Writing assessment

Think back over the extracts you have read in this chapter. Remind yourself of the vocabulary and writing techniques you have learned. Now it's time for you to put your skills into practice as you write your own autobiographical or biographical piece.

Choose one of the writing tasks opposite to complete. Whichever one you select, you should follow the same process below.

1. Consider a few ideas. Decide which you will be able to write a full piece about. Check it links clearly with your chosen task. Decide on your final choice.

2. Plan your ideas. These can be jotted down as notes or in a spider diagram. Number your ideas to make sure you know the order you will write them in.

3. Write your first draft. Try to make your writing as good as it can be, but remember that you will have the chance to revise and improve it.

4. Edit your draft.
   - Check you have used at least some of the techniques you have learned about and seen in published writers' texts.
   - Check that what you have written makes sense. It may help to read it aloud.
   - Check your spelling and punctuation.
   - Think carefully about whether your writing will inform and interest your reader.

5. Write a final version ready for assessment.

> **Tip**
> It is often helpful to read your work aloud when you are editing or proofreading.

Street food for sale!

Unit 5: Writing assessment

Choose **one** of the following writing tasks:

Task A

Write a piece of autobiography or biography about a time when you, or someone you know, did something well.

You should include:

- clear details of the setting
- a narrative that is mainly organised chronologically
- adverbs and adverbials of time to show when events happened
- paragraphs that each focus on a particular topic
- a variety of sentence types.

Task B

Write a description of a place you associate with delicious food. You might wish to use one of the photos below to give you some ideas.

You should include:

- clear details of the setting
- prepositions to locate the setting precisely
- nouns and noun phrases to give details of the food
- a variety of sentence types
- paragraphs that each focus on a particular topic.

Enjoying a meal together

121

5 Witnesses and reports

Unit 1

A terrifying experience

In this unit, you will:

- Learn how **adverbials** help to **structure** and **sequence** a text.
- Explore how thoughts and feelings can be combined with action to create effective description.
- Learn, understand and practise using new vocabulary.

By reading reports from around the world, we can share the thoughts and feelings of people who have witnessed or experienced some shocking or moving events – things that we will probably never encounter ourselves. In this chapter you will learn how writers convey information and describe their emotional reactions to events.

In 2004, a tsunami (a huge sea wave caused by an underwater earthquake) hit Thailand in South East Asia. In the following extract from her account published on a website, Laura Wales Holliday describes what it was like to be caught up in it.

Key terms

adverbial a word or phrase that gives more information about a verb, and tells you about time, place, manner or number

sequence the order in which events or ideas are written

structure how a text is ordered, the connections made between ideas and themes, and where the writer is directing the reader's focus

Ready, set, go!

As you read the extract opposite, think about how the writer uses description to help us understand the terrible things that happened to her.

Unit 1: A terrifying experience

Extract from 'Tsunami on Koh Phi Phi' by Laura Wales Holliday
454 words

Suddenly a **ferocious** wind hit the bungalow, rattling the window and shaking the palm trees outside. At the same moment, the overhead light went out. I looked out the window in time to see a dark wall of water exploding around the sides of the **bungalow** in front of ours. It appeared to be just above chest-level, and was moving with a **velocity** and roar that I'd never seen or heard before. I knew instantly what it meant. 'Oh my God, it's a tsunami!' I yelled to James as I grabbed his arm and jumped on the bed, pulling him up after me. Unfortunately, the water wasn't just chest deep. What I saw must have been the very beginning of the 20-foot wave behind it.

When the wave hit our bungalow I was ripped apart from James and never saw him again. I've never felt anything like the force of that wave. The blow was like a solid object striking each area of my body simultaneously. I was thrown backwards as the bungalow's roof and walls crashed on top of us. For a minute I simply tumbled with the water as the entire bungalow was swept inland, and then suddenly the movement stopped. Everything was dark and I was pinned down by **debris** and the weight of the water, unable to move any of my limbs. In retrospect, this must have been when my legs were **gouged** by pieces of the building, but at the time I was only aware of a general crushing sensation throughout my body. […]

If I had to die, I didn't want my last seconds to be spent scared and struggling. I relaxed my body and thought about my family. I knew how much my death would devastate them and wondered how they would cope. In my mind, I repeated over and over to my parents, 'I'm so sorry, I love you, I'm so sorry.' Then finally I couldn't stand the pain any longer. There was nothing I could do but the urge to breathe was so intense that I opened my mouth and started **inhaling** the water. I can still remember the gritty taste of the water, full of sand and concrete. I wanted nothing more than for the pain to stop, and after a few moments it did. As my lungs filled, my vision went from blurry darkness to pure white. The weight of the water seemed to disappear and I felt light again. I was a moment away from either unconsciousness or death.

Before either occurred, another wave hit and something that was trapping me suddenly shifted. I gave one instinctive kick and suddenly my head was above water and I gulped a breath of air.

---

ferocious – fierce
bungalow – a single-storey house
velocity – speed
debris – scattered pieces of rubbish or remains
gouged – made a hole
inhaling – breathing in

Damage caused by the tsunami that hit Koh Phi Phi in 2004

5.1 Chapter 5: Witnesses and reports

⚡ Word power

Re-read the extract on page 123. Pay particular attention to the target words listed below. As you read, think about what each of the words might mean in the extract.

Your target words for this section are:

- simultaneously
- retrospect
- sensation
- devastate
- instinctive

These target words have been highlighted in blue in the extract on page 123.

The boat tipped over!

1 The word 'simultaneously' is an **adverb** that means 'at the same time'.

   a. Add the word 'simultaneously' to the following sentences.

   The boat tipped over and Sarah gave a cry.

   The football match was broadcast on TV and it was also broadcast on the radio.

   b. Write a sentence of your own, using the word 'simultaneously'.

> **Tip** ✓
>
> Remember that many adverbs can be placed in different positions in a sentence. Experiment and decide which position you think is the most effective.

2 The word 'retrospect' is often used with the word 'in' to form an adverb phrase, meaning 'looking back'. It is often coupled with the phrase 'but at the time'. Look at this sentence from the article:

> 'In retrospect, this must have been when my legs were gouged by pieces of the building, but at the time I was only aware of a general crushing sensation throughout my body.'

Use this sentence as a model for a sentence of your own in which you describe the effect of an accident.

3 The word 'sensation' has more than one meaning. Look it up in the Target word list on pages 174–175 and decide which of the two definitions is being used in the extract. Be prepared to explain your decision.

124

Unit 1: A terrifying experience

4 The word 'devastate' means to totally destroy or overwhelm, for example *The city was devastated by an earthquake*. In the extract, Wales Holliday says:

> 'I knew how much my death would devastate them [her parents].'

Explain why 'devastate' is such an effective word choice in this sentence.

Key terms

adjective a word that describes a person, place, object or sound

adverb a word that gives more detail about a verb, an adjective or another adverb

noun a word used to name a place, person, feeling, thing or idea

5 The **adjective** 'instinctive' comes from the **noun** 'instinct', which means something that we do naturally, without thinking. We can also use it as an adverb – 'instinctively'. Add the adjective or the adverb to the following sentences.

> I crossed to the other side of the road to avoid them.

> He didn't have to train; he was a natural dancer.

Knowledge and understanding

Look back at the extract on page 123 and answer the following questions.

1 What was the first sign that a tsunami was about to happen?

2 In the second paragraph, what situation does Wales Holliday find herself in when the bungalow stops moving?

3 In the third paragraph, why does she decide to relax?

4 At the end of the third paragraph, she says 'I felt light again'. Which of the following was actually happening to her?

She was saved.   She was feeling happier.

She was beginning to drown.

125

Chapter 5: Witnesses and reports

5.1

✏️ Writing skills

1 The events that Wales Holliday describes happened quickly. Look at how she constructs the sentence below to help the reader follow the sequence of events.

She starts with an adverb of time to help us understand the pace of the events. Then she adds two **clauses** introduced by **conjunctions** to show us the order of the events.

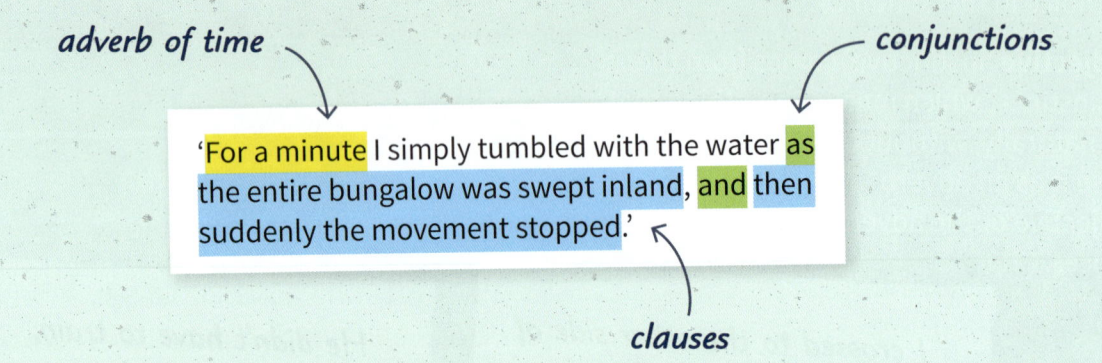

adverb of time — *conjunctions*

'**For a minute** I simply tumbled with the water **as** the entire bungalow was swept inland, **and** then suddenly the movement stopped.'

clauses

Use the information below about a bicycle accident to write a sentence like the one above, including these words: *for a minute, as, and*. Change or add words until you are happy that the sentence works.

My front wheel hit a pothole.

I was confused.

I was thrown from my bicycle.

What happened in the bicycle accident?

Unit 1: A terrifying experience

2 Wales Holliday starts three of her paragraphs with adverbial clauses (for example, 'When the wave hit our bungalow…'). These guide the reader through the events by linking one paragraph to the next, like this:

final sentence of the first paragraph

'What I saw must have been the very beginning of the 20-foot wave behind it. When the wave hit our bungalow…'

adverb clause linked to 'the 20-foot wave' in the previous paragraph

Now try this for yourself. Here is the last sentence of a paragraph about a cycling accident.

> I was daydreaming and so I didn't notice **the enormous pothole** until it was too late.

Write the opening sentence to the next paragraph, starting with an adverb clause (beginning with *when* or *as*) linked to the highlighted **noun phrase**.

3 One of the reasons this piece of writing is so effective is that, alongside her description of the action, Wales Holliday includes her thoughts and feelings. For example:

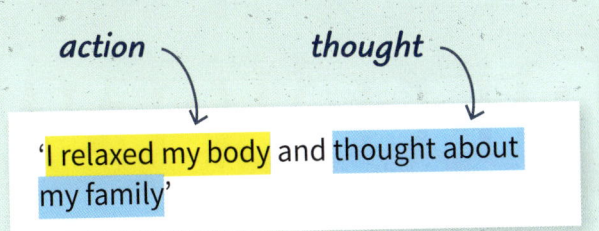

action   *thought*

'I relaxed my body and thought about my family'

Add another sentence to your writing about the bicycle accident, in which you link an action with a thought or feeling.

Key terms

clause a group of words with a verb

conjunction a linking word that joins words or groups of words together, e.g. *if*, *but*, *and*

noun phrase a group of words that has a noun as its head or key word. All the words in the group tell us more about the head noun, e.g. *a big muddy puddle* ('puddle' is the head noun)

❗ Check your skills

Imagine you have witnessed a natural disaster and write an account of your experience.

- Group the events into three or four paragraphs to describe them in sequence.
- Begin each paragraph with an adverbial that links to the previous paragraph.
- Link your actions to your thoughts and feelings.

Remember to check the spelling, punctuation and grammar of your writing.

127

5.2 Chapter 5: Witnesses and reports

Unit 2

Discovery!

In this unit, you will:

- Explain how a writer's use of **sentence structure** and release of information controls **narrative pace** and builds **suspense**.

- Explore how verbs, adjectives and **figurative language** are used to convey a discovery.

- Learn, understand and practise using new vocabulary.

We aren't all lucky enough to discover hidden treasure but, by reading a first-hand account, we can get very close.

On 26 November 1922, Howard Carter made one of the most important archaeological discoveries of the 20th century. In the Valley of the Kings, he unearthed the tomb of an ancient Egyptian pharaoh, a boy-king named Tutankhamen. In this extract from his account of the expedition, he describes the moment when he first saw the tomb.

Ready, set, go!

As you read the extract opposite, think about how Carter helps us to understand how impressive his discovery was.

Key terms

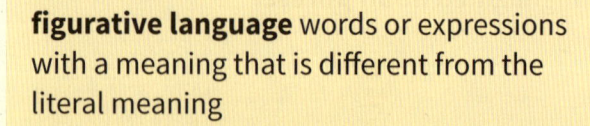

figurative language words or expressions with a meaning that is different from the literal meaning

narrative pace the speed at which the action of a story moves along

sentence structure how a sentence is put together, including word and punctuation choices and word order

suspense an anxious or uncertain feeling while waiting for something to happen or become known

Unit 2: Discovery!

Extract from *The Discovery of the Tomb of Tutankhamen* by Howard Carter and A. C. Mace
451 words

Feverishly we cleared away the remaining last scraps of rubbish on the floor of the passage before the doorway, until we had only the clean sealed doorway before us. In this, after making preliminary notes, we made a tiny **breach** in the top left-hand corner to see what was beyond. Darkness and the iron **testing rod** told us that there was empty space. Perhaps another descending staircase, in accordance with the ordinary royal **Theban** tomb plan? Or maybe a chamber? Candles were **procured** – the all important tell-tale for foul gases when opening an ancient **subterranean** excavation – I widened the breach and by means of the candle looked in, while Ld. C., Lady E. and Callender, with the Reises, waited in anxious expectation.

It was sometime before one could see, the hot air escaping caused the candle to flicker, but as soon as one's eyes became accustomed to the glimmer of light the interior of the chamber gradually loomed before one, with its strange and wonderful **medley** of extraordinary and beautiful objects heaped upon one another.

There was naturally some suspense for those present who could not see, when Lord Carnarvon said to me, 'Can you see anything?' I replied to him, 'Yes, it is wonderful.' I then with precaution made the hole sufficiently large for both of us to see. With the light of an electric torch, as well as an additional candle, we looked in. Our sensations and astonishment are difficult to describe as the better light revealed to us the marvellous collection of treasures: two strange ebony-black **effigies** of a King, gold sandalled, loomed out from the cloak of darkness; strange black shrines with a gilded monster snake appearing from within; quite ordinary-looking white chests; finely carved chairs; a golden inlaid throne; […] beneath our very eyes, on the threshold, a lovely […] wishing-cup; stools of all shapes and designs, of both common and rare materials; and, lastly, a confusion of overturned parts of chariots glinting with gold, peering from amongst which was a **mannikin**. The first impression of which suggested the **property-room** of an opera of a vanished civilisation. Our sensations were bewildering and full of strange emotion. We questioned one another as to the meaning of it all. Was it a tomb or merely a **cache**? A sealed doorway between the two sentinel statues proved there was more beyond, and with the numerous **cartouches** bearing the name of Tut.ankh.Amen on most of the objects before us, there was little doubt that there behind was the grave of that Pharaoh.

We closed the hole, locked the wooden grill which had been placed upon the first doorway, we mounted our donkeys and return[ed] home, contemplating what we had seen.

---

breach – hole
testing rod – a long iron rod, which can be poked into a hole to see how deep it is
Theban – from the ancient city of Thebes in Egypt
procured – fetched or got
subterranean – underground
medley – mixture
effigies – sculptures or models of people
mannikin – a model of the human body
property-room – a room where theatre companies keep their props, the objects and furniture that will be on the stage
cache – a hidden store of valuable things
cartouches – symbols that represent the name of an Ancient Egyptian king

5.2 Chapter 5: Witnesses and reports

⚡ Word power

Re-read the extract on page 129. Pay particular attention to the target words listed below. As you read, think about what each of the words might mean in the extract.

Your target words for this section are:

- preliminary
- accustomed
- precaution
- sentinel
- contemplating

These target words have been highlighted in blue in the extract on page 129.

The cartouche (carved tablet) for Tutankhamen

1 Find the word 'preliminary' in the extract. Choose the closest **synonym** from the following words.

| detailed | final | initial |

✓ Tip

What does the **prefix** 'pre-' usually mean? Prefixes can often give you useful clues to the meaning of unknown words. Make sure that you know what these common prefixes usually mean: *pre-, dis-, re-*.

📖 Key terms

prefix a word or group of letters placed in front of another word to add to or change its meaning

synonym a word that means the same or almost the same as another word, e.g. 'glad' is a synonym for 'happy'

2 Think again about the meaning of the prefix 'pre-', then add 'caution' to make the word 'precaution'.

a. What might it mean? Look at how the word 'precaution' is used in the extract. Check your answer in the Target word list on pages 174–175.

b. Now complete the following sentence to include the word 'precaution':

It didn't look as if it was going to rain, but...

130

Unit 2: Discovery!

3 In the following sentence, the word 'used' could be replaced by 'accustomed'.

> My eyes were now used to the darkness.

Complete the following sentence to include the word 'accustomed'.

> I am so… that I don't miss the central heating at all.

4 Re-read the final sentence of the extract and look up 'contemplating' in the Target word list on pages 174–175. Decide which of the following photos shows a person contemplating and explain your choice.

💡 Knowledge and understanding

Re-read the sentence containing 'sentinel'. A sentinel is a guard. What do you think the statues were guarding and why? Look back at the extract on page 129 and answer the following questions.

1 Which word in the first sentence tells us that Carter and his team were very keen to get to the door?

2 After making the hole in the door, why did Carter decide to light candles? Give two reasons.

3 In the third paragraph, Carter says:

> 'There was naturally some suspense for those present who could not see'

Why couldn't the others see inside the room?

4 In the third paragraph, Carter tells us that:

> 'Our sensations were bewildering and full of strange emotion.'

Explain why you think they were feeling like this.

5 In the third paragraph, what did they see that told them that this was Tutankhamen's tomb?

131

5.2 Chapter 5: Witnesses and reports

📖 Reading skills

1 Re-read the first paragraph and look at how Carter slows down the narrative pace of his account and delays telling us what he saw when he looked into the tomb. This builds the suspense because we want to know what he saw.

Here is a section of that first paragraph. Notice how he uses questions and **parenthesis** (marked by **dashes**) to lengthen the sentences so that we feel that, like the other members of the team, we're trying to look over his shoulder.

He releases a little information to raise our expectations.

Questions build up our expectations of what he may find. 'Perhaps' and 'maybe' show hope and uncertainty.

> 'Darkness and the iron testing rod told us that there was empty space. Perhaps another descending staircase, in accordance with the ordinary royal Theban tomb plan? Or maybe a chamber? Candles were procured – the all important tell-tale for foul gases when opening an ancient subterranean excavation – I widened the breach and by means of the candle looked in, while Ld. C., Lady E. and Callender, with the Reises, waited in anxious expectation.'

The parenthesis with dashes adds to the length of the sentence, increasing the suspense by slowing the pace.

We are told how the others were reacting and waiting so that we identify with them.

Information is withheld, not saying what he saw until the end of the next paragraph.

Use the annotations and any ideas of your own to complete the following sentences explaining how Carter creates suspense in this section of his account. Support your points with quotations and references to the text.

> *Carter begins by telling us only that... Instead, he... This makes us...*

132

Unit 2: Discovery!

2 After the suspense of the first two paragraphs, Carter knows that he must describe the tomb's contents very vividly or we'll feel disappointed.

Re-read the section from 'Our sensations and astonishment are difficult to describe…' (line 16) to '… vanished civilisation' (line 24). This is a long list, broken up by **semi-colons**. Look closely at the way Carter has chosen his language to impress the reader in the example below.

Copy the extract below and annotate it, identifying the descriptive language (especially the verb and adjectives) and explain what effects they have.

> 'strange black shrines with a gilded monster snake appearing from within; quite ordinary-looking white chests; finely carved chairs; a golden inlaid throne'

more adjectives, this time including bright, contrasting colour

powerful, precise adjectives

> 'two strange ebony-black effigies of a King, gold sandalled, loomed out from the cloak of darkness'

striking verb, suggesting that the statues have come to life

metaphor, reminding us there is more, hidden in the dark. It makes the gold stand out in the reader's mind, creating a threatening image.

Key terms

dash a punctuation mark (–) used to show a pause

metaphor describing something as something else, not meant to be taken literally, e.g. *You are a star*

parenthesis an extra piece of information added to a sentence, usually marked off by brackets, dashes or commas

semi-colon a punctuation mark (;) often used to divide up detailed items in a list

How effective is the mention of candles?

! Check your skills

Explain how Carter builds suspense in the second paragraph, commenting on:
- how he holds back and releases information
- how he structures the sentence
- any words or phrases that slow down the pace to create suspense.

133

5.3 Chapter 5: Witnesses and reports

Unit 3

Reporting the world

In this unit, you will:

- Learn how **direct quotation** and reported speech can be used effectively.
- Explore how language and structure can be used to create emotion in a report.
- Learn, understand and practise using new vocabulary.

According to the environmental organisation Greenpeace, an estimated 12.7 million tonnes of plastic – everything from plastic bottles and bags to microbeads – end up in our oceans each year. That's one truck-load of rubbish every minute. The web magazine report opposite describes the effect this has on one island in the Pacific Ocean.

Key term

direct quotation the presentation inside inverted commas of actual words spoken, e.g. "I'm hungry," the child complained to her father.

Ready, set, go!

As you read the extract opposite, think about how the reporter wants you to feel about this news story.

Unit 3: Reporting the world

Extract from 'A Remote Paradise Island Is Now a Plastic Junkyard',
The Atlantic, 15 May 2017
472 words

Henderson Island is about the most remote place you can visit without leaving the planet. It sits squarely in the middle of the South Pacific, 3,500 miles from New Zealand in one direction and another 3,500 miles from South America in the other. To get there, Jennifer Lavers (from the Institute for Marine & Antarctic Studies, University of Tasmania) had to fly from Tasmania to Tahiti, catch a small, once-a-week plane to the Gambier Islands, join a freight ship that had already sailed for 10 days from New Zealand, and ask it to change course for Henderson. No ship travels there unless you specifically ask it to.

And yet, somehow, Google Street View has been there. Lavers took virtual strolls along two of the island's beaches before she made her epic journey. That's when she realised just how much plastic there is.

You can see for yourself. Pull Henderson Island up on Google Maps and drag the yellow **avatar** to the bottom of the eastern beach. Now, start walking. It starts unobtrusively: a bottle here, a bit of tubing there. But soon, the scraps pile up until the sand is carpeted in multi-coloured junk.

When Lavers actually arrived on Henderson, she found that the situation was even worse than the images had suggested. At her landing site, her team immediately came across a truck tyre – so large and deeply buried that they couldn't move it. 'That was a warning,' she said. 'It got worse and worse. There's an area that we call the garbage patch, where you can't put your foot down without stepping on a bottle cap. The sheer **volume** really took my breath away for all the wrong reasons.'

Henderson should be pristine. It is uninhabited. Tourists don't go there. There's no one around to drop any litter. The whole place was declared a World Heritage Site by the United Nations in 1988. The nearest settlement is 71 miles away, and has just 40 people on it. And yet, **seafaring** plastic has turned it into yet another of humanity's scrapheaps. 'It's truly one of the last **paradises** left on earth, and one of the least visited but heavily protected bits of land on the planet,' Lavers says. 'But I don't think I've stood somewhere and been so utterly and completely surrounded by plastic.'

The team found several purple **hermit crabs** that had taken to shoving their bodies in junk, using bottle caps and other **detritus in lieu** of seashells. Other island residents weren't so lucky; at least one sea turtle had become fatally entangled in fishing line. And the team themselves struggled to cope. 'After a while, your brain has to shut off,' says Lavers. 'You focus on things like a toy soldier or some dice – something that reminds you of something fun from your childhood. That's the **coping mechanism.**'

---

avatar – an image that represents you online
volume – amount
seafaring – regularly travelling by sea
paradise – an ideal or perfect place
hermit crabs – crabs that usually live in the cast-off shells of sea snails

detritus – waste or debris
in lieu – instead
coping mechanism – way of dealing with stress or difficult situations

5.3 Chapter 5: Witnesses and reports

Word power

Re-read the extract on page 135. Pay particular attention to the target words listed below. As you read, think about what each of the words might mean in the extract.

Your target words for this section are:

- specifically
- epic
- unobtrusively
- carpeted
- pristine

These target words have been highlighted in blue in the text on page 135.

A carpet of flowers!

1. Look up 'specifically' in the Target word list on pages 174–175. Now use it in two sentences, one each to describe the following situations:
   - You ask a courier to deliver a parcel before midday because you have to go out.
   - You order a meal at a restaurant without chips but the waiter brings it with chips.

2. An 'epic' was originally a long poem narrating the deeds and adventures of heroic figures or the past history of a nation. It is used as an adjective in the extract. What does the word tell us about Lavers' journey?

3. Look up 'unobtrusively' in the target word list on pages 174–175. Which of the following people might need to walk through a crowd unobtrusively:

   a spy   a pickpocket

   a street entertainer   a market trader

   Explain your choices.

4. Usually, we think of a carpet as a soft fabric covering for a floor. Look at the way the word 'carpeted' is used in the extract.

   a. What does the word tell us about the plastic waste?

   b. Use the word 'carpeted' in a sentence describing a woodland clearing in autumn or spring.

Unit 3: Reporting the world

5. Look up the word 'pristine' in the Target word list on pages 174–175.

   a. Which of the following words are **antonyms** for 'pristine'?

   - expensive
   - soiled
   - beautiful
   - tatty

   b. What do you or your family own – or would like to own – that you would want to keep in pristine condition? Explain what it is and why.

> **Key term**
>
> **antonym** a word meaning the opposite of another word, e.g. 'good' and 'bad' are antonyms of each other

Hermit crabs use plastic cups as shells.

Knowledge and understanding

Look back at the extract on page 135 and answer the following questions.

1. Why does Jennifer Lavers have to ask the ship's captain to take her to Henderson Island?

2. Which two of the following statements are true?
   - Henderson Island is uninhabited.
   - No one has ever been there before.
   - People go there on holiday.
   - You can see images of the island on the internet.

   Support your decisions with evidence from the text.

3. How does all the plastic rubbish get to Henderson Island?

4. Lavers says that when she saw the part of the island called the garbage patch, 'The sheer volume really took my breath away for all the wrong reasons.' Writers usually use the term 'took my breath away' to convey their wonder or amazement when viewing a beautiful scene. How is it used here?

5. Find two examples of the impact that the rubbish has had on the island's wildlife.

6. Lavers is obviously very saddened and worried by the state of the island. Re-read the final paragraph and explain how she deals with her emotions while she is on the island.

5.3 Chapter 5: Witnesses and reports

✏️ Writing skills

1 In newspaper reports, journalists often include direct quotations from interviews with people who are involved in the story.

> '"That was a warning," she said.' ⟵ *direct quotation*

Here are three likely reasons why the journalist included direct quotations from Jennifer Lavers in this text:

- Hearing Lavers' voice makes the report more convincing because she has first-hand experience of the island.
- Her words add emotion to the factual information.
- She is an expert in marine studies and so we believe what she says.

Select one quote from the extract and explain why you think the journalist included it. Explain what effect it has on the reader.

2 a. Rewrite the following sentence as direct speech:

> In a separate interview Henderson Island, Jennifer Lavers said that she was so appalled by the amount of plastic in the oceans that she had taken to using a bamboo iPhone case and toothbrush.

Think carefully about the most effective punctuation to end the quotation and explain your choice.

b. Which of the following statements could be used to introduce your quotation? Choose one and be prepared to explain your choice:

- Her experience has made Lavers change her own behaviour.
- Lavers only uses bamboo toothbrushes.
- Lavers owns an iPhone.

c. Where could you insert this new statement and quotation into the extract? Explain your decision.

> **Tip** ✓
>
> Remember to change the tense of the verb in what Lavers said and to include 'says Lavers' or similar.

Unit 3: **Reporting the world**

3 Look at how the journalist makes his viewpoint clear by contrasting the remoteness and beauty of the island with the ugliness and destructive power of the plastic. Re-read the following section:

'Henderson should be pristine. It is uninhabited. Tourists don't go there. There's no one around to drop any litter. The whole place was declared a World Heritage Site by the United Nations in 1988. The nearest settlement is 71 miles away, and has just 40 people on it. And yet, seafaring plastic has turned it into yet another of humanity's scrapheaps.'

Notice how the first six sentences (highlighted in blue) describe the island in positive terms, creating a perfect picture in our minds. This makes the final sentence (highlighted in yellow) more shocking and emotionally powerful.

Try this structure for yourself. Imagine that you are walking in a beautiful wood and you suddenly come across a pile of rubbish. Use the extract above as a model to help you write a paragraph of at least four sentences that contrasts the beauty of the wood with the ugliness of the rubbish. Make the final sentence pack an emotional punch.

Tip

Notice how the journalist has used some short, simple sentences. These create a rhythm and add to the emotional power of the final sentence.

How does this pile of rubbish make you feel?

Check your skills

Write one or two paragraphs based on information in the text in which you express your own views about the dangers of plastic rubbish. Appeal to your readers' emotions, thinking carefully about how you want them to feel.

Use Henderson Island as an example and include at least one direct quotation from Jennifer Lavers to support your views.

Remember to check your work for grammar, punctuation and spelling mistakes.

5.4 Chapter 5: Witnesses and reports

Unit 4

Writing from the heart

In this unit, you will:

- Explore the purpose and audience of a diary.
- Explore how a writer uses the diary form to convey powerful ideas and emotions in a simple way.
- Learn, understand and practise using new vocabulary.

All wars cause terrible suffering and it is often difficult for soldiers to talk about their experiences. One young officer in the First World War, Charlie May, decided to write his thoughts down in a diary, which he addressed to his wife. In the extract on page 141, he describes some of his experiences and feelings while in the trenches.

Ready, set, go!

As you read the extract, think about why Charlie May might have wanted to keep a diary and why he decided to address it to his wife.

Extract from *To Fight Alongside Friends: The First World War Diaries Of Charlie May*, edited by Gerry Harrison
349 words

January 13, 1916

I long and long to see you, to clasp you in my arms […] and I long with all my heart to see my Baby. How I love her. What hopes I have for her, what a sweet girl she will make.

February 25, 1916

Woke up this morning to find the snow pelting down and covering the ground fully five inches deep.

Also it was freezing hard. Cotton [a fellow officer] came in to breakfast with us. He brought the little bible which [another soldier] had taken from the body of the dead German.

On the **fly-leaf** in a child's handwriting the word Dada.

War is very sad.

Perhaps the man may have been something to loathe and detest. I do not know. All I am conscious of is that somewhere in his **fatherland** there is a little child who called him Dada.

April 6, 1916

Fritz strafed our new trenches with heavies and searched round the support with HE (high-explosive) **shrapnel** and other such obnoxious stuff.

One shell claimed three **NCOs** and wounded three men. We all feel wild to get at the beast and hope we may string him up on the wire. I saw the killed go down the line. It was a pitiful sight.

Poor boys, shell fire is a horrid thing.

Gresty – a lad who was a sergeant of mine – was the worst […] It was very, very sad.

Do those at home realise how their boys go out for them? Never can they do enough for their soldiers, never can they repay the debt they owe. […]

June 17, 1916

I do not want to die… the thought that I may never see you or our darling baby again turns my bowels to water.

My conscience is clear that I have always tried to make life a joy for you. But it is the thought that our babe may grow up without my knowing her and without her knowing me. I pray God I may do my duty for I know whatever that may entail you would not have it otherwise.

---

fly-leaf – the page at the front of a book with nothing printed on it
fatherland – like 'motherland', this is a way of referring to where a person was born
Fritz – an insulting nickname used by British soldiers in the First World War to refer to German soldiers
strafed – attacked them with a lot of bullets or bombs
shrapnel – sharp pieces of metal that fly out of an exploding bomb
NCOs – non-commissioned officers, the lowest officer rank in the army

How does knowing the German had a child make Charlie feel?

5.4 Chapter 5: Witnesses and reports

⚡ Word power

Re-read the extract on page 141. Pay particular attention to the target words listed below. As you read, think about what each of the words might mean in the extract.

Your target words for this section are:

- long
- detest
- obnoxious
- conscience
- entail

These target words have been highlighted in blue in the extract on page 141.

1 When the word 'long' is used as a verb, it means to have a strong wish. Complete these sentences, including a form of the verb 'to long'.

> The night before her birthday she lay awake…

> The whole of the time he was in prison, he…

2 Look at how the word 'detest' is used in the extract. Which of the following is an antonym for 'detest'?

   admire   hate   ignore

3 The word 'obnoxious' means extremely unpleasant.

   a. Which of the following words is a synonym for 'obnoxious' as it is used in the extract?

   revolting   annoying   irritating

   b. Write a short description of someone behaving in a way that you consider to be obnoxious. Use the word in your description.

Unit 4: Writing from the heart

4 Our conscience tells us if we are doing right or wrong. Write a paragraph about someone being tempted to shoplift. Include the word 'conscience' in your writing.

5 The word 'entail' means something you can't avoid. Use a form of the word 'entail' to complete the following sentences:

> I didn't want to take the bus because that…

> Applying online is annoying because it…

Is she tempted?

💡 Knowledge and understanding

Look back at the extract on page 141 and answer the following questions.

1 Find and copy down a word from the diary entry for January 13, 1916 that means to hold tightly. What does this tell us about May's feelings?

2 Re-read the diary entry for February 25, 1916.
  a. What does Charlie May see that makes him feel sad?
  b. Explain why it has this effect on him.

3 At the end of the diary entry for April 6, 1916, May says:

> 'Do those at home realise how their boys go out for them? Never can they do enough for their soldiers, never can they repay the debt they owe.'

In your own words, explain what you think he means.

4 In the diary entry for June 17, 1916, May expresses his fears and hopes. What are they?

First World War memorial

143

5.4 Chapter 5: Witnesses and reports

📖 Reading skills

1 Most diaries are private and meant to be read by one person. When a diary is published, it can be read by anyone.

Here are some statements made by students after they read the extract. Some statements are in favour of publication; others are not. Copy and complete the grid below, putting the statements on the right in appropriate columns.

In favour of publication	Against publication
	Diaries contain private thoughts.

We can learn so much about history by reading a diary like this.

It helps us understand what it's like to be a soldier.

Charlie May only ever wanted his wife to read his diary.

It's too violent.

Maybe if more people read diaries like this, they'd be less likely to go to war.

2 Re-read the diary entry for February 25, 1916. The entry starts with a simple recording of the weather but ends in a deeply moving reflection on the nature of war.

Use the annotations below and your own ideas to write a paragraph explaining what makes this entry so emotionally powerful.

Sets the scene. 'Pelting' sounds harsh. This isn't pretty snow.

The word 'hard' sounds even more uncomfortable.

Gives a simple emotional statement, stated as a fact on a separate line. Has he just thought this?

> 'Woke up this morning to find the snow pelting down and covering the ground fully five inches deep. Also it was freezing hard. Cotton [a fellow officer] came in to breakfast with us. He brought the little bible which [another soldier] had taken from the body of the dead German. On the fly-leaf in a child's handwriting the word Dada. War is very sad. Perhaps the man may have been something to loathe and detest. I do not know. All I am conscious of is that somewhere in his fatherland there is a little child who called him Dada.'

Gives just facts, no commentary. but the child's inscription is very moving. Why?

'Perhaps' and 'may' show uncertainty. Why is he uncertain?

This is very sad. It reminds us of the first entry and his longing to see his own child.

Unit 4: Writing from the heart

3 May has conflicting feelings towards the enemy.

  a. Here are the words he uses to describe them:

  - something to loathe and detest
  - Dada
  - Fritz
  - the beast

Copy and complete the table below, placing each description next to the appropriate effect.

Effect	Description
An insulting description that makes them seem silly and unimportant	
Describes them as beloved family men	
Makes them seem like wild animals	
Makes them seem like objects to be hated	

  b. Now use these ideas to write a paragraph explaining May's attitude to German soldiers, quoting the extract.

> **Tip** ✓
> Use 'on the one hand', and 'on the other hand' or 'however', to indicate the differing attitudes.

! Check your skills

Who did Charlie May want to read his diary?

Re-read the entry for April 6, 1916. Write a paragraph explaining how May reacts.

Comment on:

- how he describes the terrible event
- how he reacts to it emotionally
- what he thinks and how he expresses his thoughts.

Remember to support your ideas with quotations from the diary entry.

145

5.5 Chapter 5: Witnesses and reports

Unit 5
Reading assessment

In the following extract, Sandra Millers Younger describes her experience of surviving California's Cedar Fire of 2003. This terrible fire destroyed 2820 buildings and killed 15 people.

Read the extract below and then answer the questions that follow it. Remember to use the skills you have developed through the chapter to help you to answer these questions.

Extract from *The Fire Outside my Window* by Sandra Millers Younger
396 words

At first I resented the alarm in my husband's voice. 'Whoa! It's time to get out of here.' I was so asleep. Why was he waking me? What could possibly be so important? I opened my eyes to a strange yellow light. What was going on? In another instant I understood. The canyon was on fire. Perfectly framed by our open **draperies,** a huge **swath** of flames stretched across the mountain opposite us. At its edges, fountains of fire shot high above the ground, surging and swaying in a ragged dance, vivid orange against surrounding darkness. 'Oh my God!' I reached for a pair of jeans thrown across the foot of the bed and pulled them on. 'What do we do?'

100 words

How would you react in this situation, do you think?

'Don't panic,' Bob said, but his voice sounded thin and forced. 'We do what we need to do. First get some clothes. We don't know when we'll be able to come back.'

He turned on the lights and disappeared into the bathroom. I opened a dresser drawer, grabbed some underwear, put on a pair of socks, and then dashed into the closet and stood for a moment looking at the line of hanging clothes. What should I take? My mind couldn't focus. Fire. There was fire outside the windows. I ran back and looked out again, as if to make sure. This time I noticed an orange glow deep below us, near the entrance to our neighborhood road. A spike of electricity surged through me as I pieced it all together.

200 words

146

Unit 5: Reading assessment

The flames on the mountain across from us must be only part of a bigger fire, a massive beast closing in.

'Bob, it's on our side!' I said, my throat closing around the words.

> 300 words

He was standing by the bed over an open suitcase, but rushed to join me.

'It's on our side,' he repeated, almost in a whisper.

At that moment, something shifted inside me. A **distinct** sensation. Bob felt it, too. We talked about it later, how thinking and doing slammed together in an instant, in a rush of **adrenaline**. From then on we were caught up in a current of pure instinct, obeying without question some kind of primitive **knowing** that moved us step by step toward safety, kept us from lingering too long on any one task. Above all, we knew we had to leave. We should have left already.

> 400 words

---

draperies – curtains
swath (also spelled swathe) – a broad strip or area of something
distinct – clear and different
adrenaline – a chemical in the body that is released when someone is excited, stressed or frightened
knowing – knowledge (in this context)

---

1 In the first sentence, find and identify a word that tells us that Millers Younger was annoyed by the way her husband woke her.

2 Re-read from 'What was going on?' (line 6) to the end of the first paragraph. How does Millers Younger convey her discovery of the fire? Comment on the following:
- the language she uses to describe the fire (especially verbs and adjectives)
- figurative language
- her spoken words.

3 In the second paragraph, she describes her husband's voice as sounding 'thin and forced'. What does this tell you about how he was feeling?

4 How does Millers Younger control the pace and build suspense in the third paragraph from 'My mind couldn't focus' (lines 23–24) to the end of the paragraph? Comment on:
- sentence structure
- how she withholds and releases information.

5 Re-read the final paragraph. Miller Younger says:

> 'At that moment, something shifted inside me.'

She then explains how she and her husband felt and acted differently from this moment on. In your own words, explain how their actions, thoughts and feelings changed.

147

6 Viewpoints and issues

Unit 1

Speaking my mind (1)

In this unit, you will:

- Explore how **sentence structure** and language choices add to the effectiveness of an argument.
- Explore how a writer presents evidence to support their argument.
- Learn, understand and practise using new vocabulary.

There are times when all of us feel so strongly about something that we feel we must express our views – to make others see what we see. This may be prompted by our own experiences or by something we have read about or seen in the media. In this chapter, you will read a selection of outspoken writing, ranging from an anonymous blogger to a Victorian servant. You will also learn how to express your own views powerfully and effectively.

Fed up with what she saw as unfair portrayal in the press and on TV, 'Sgt Ellie Bloggs' wanted to tell the world about what it is *really* like to be a frontline police officer. She set up an anonymous blog to write about her experiences. In the extract on page 149, she explains why she thinks we need to spend more money on the police.

Key term

sentence structure how a sentence is put together, including word and punctuation choices and word order

Ready, set, go!

As you read the extract opposite, think about the impression you get of the work that police officers do.

Unit 1: Speaking my mind (1)

Extract from 'Off With Stress' by Sgt Ellie Bloggs
414 words

At last, some concrete figures to support what **front-line** officers have been feeling over the last few years: police officers off sick with stress is up a whopping 35% in flat numbers despite a decrease in overall police numbers.

When I joined Blandshire Constabulary in 2003, there was never a shortage of people putting their hands up for **voluntary overtime**, to stay on dealing with shoplifters, doing scene watches, or just covering shortages on the next shift. In recent years as a sergeant, trying to find people to stay on was like pulling teeth. In the end, we'd just **draw straws**. Gruelling **shift patterns**, reduced staffing levels and reduction in rest day working payments, have all contributed.

All these measures were designed to save money and alter police conditions to bring it more in line with a 'normal' job. Instead, they are forcing overtime budgets up and now we are seeing the consequence of trying to treat police officers like any other employees.

Police work is not 'normal'. That's not me having an inflated view of myself or my colleagues. That's fact. In any other job, if someone swears in your face and threatens you, you call a manager or for the police. If there's a fire alarm or bomb alert, you evacuate to safety. If a colleague is attacked and seriously injured, someone else will come to help you and deal with it.

In the police, you are the one that deals with these situations. I have tended to injured **parties** while fights go on around my head. I have been assaulted and threatened on numerous occasions. I have reassured people who were dying, even though it was hopeless. I have crept alone through darkened houses looking for intruders, because the householders were too afraid. […] I have taken decisions that no one else wanted to take, when all my managers were asleep in bed. I have been blamed for mistakes I've made and the mistakes of others. I have seen good men and women drawn to desperate acts that lost them their jobs, due to a lack of supervision and support.

Policing is not a normal job, but it is done by normal humans. The moment you forget that, police officers will lack the support and respect needed to stay motivated, healthy, and honest. If you think that's an excuse, show me that you would be any different.

Like it or lump it, we will get the police force we pay for.

---

front-line – dealing directly with the public
voluntary overtime – extra hours that an employee chooses to work on top of their normal contracted hours. Often these are paid at a higher rate than normal hours
draw straws – decide something by picking at random from straws of different lengths
shift patterns – working arrangements, e.g. two early shifts (07:00–15:00), followed by two late shifts (15:00–23:00) and two night shifts (22:00–07:00) with three rest days before starting the pattern again
parties – a legal term for people
like it or lump it – whether you like it or not

Are we asking police officers to cope with too much?

6.1 Chapter 6: Viewpoints and issues

⚡ Word power

Re-read the extract on page 149. Pay particular attention to the target words listed below. As you read, think about what the words might mean in this extract.

Your target words for this section are:

- concrete
- gruelling
- inflated
- desperate
- motivated

These target words have been highlighted in blue in the extract on page 149.

> **Key term**
>
> **adjective** a word that describes a person, place, object or sound

1. Concrete is a hard substance used in the construction of buildings and roads, but the word can also be used to describe anything real that isn't just an idea. Look at how it is used in the opening sentence of the blog post.

Complete these sentences using the word 'concrete' in the same way.

> *I don't want to hear any more of your vague ideas, I want… !*

> *There's no point in you accusing me of the crime, unless you have…*

2. In the 19th century, prisoners were given gruel (watery, tasteless porridge or soup) to eat. This led to the word 'gruel' being used as an **adjective** – 'gruelling' – to describe any horrible punishment. Find it in the extract and explain what it means there.

3. We inflate a bicycle tyre by pumping it full of air. Look at how the word 'inflated' is used in the extract. What do you think it means there? Use the Target word list on pages 174–175 to check the different meanings of this word.

What does a bicycle tyre look like when it's pumped up?

150

Unit 1: Speaking my mind (1)

4 If you act desperately, you are under so much pressure that you don't care what the consequences of your actions might be. Which of the actions below might be thought of as desperate acts?

- Walking out of your job
- Running away from home
- Asking a friend for advice

5 When you are motivated, you want to take action. Which of the following words is closest in meaning?

- relaxed
- uninterested
- keen

Knowledge and understanding

Look back at the extract on page 149 and answer the following questions.

1 Has the number of police officers off sick with stress increased or decreased recently?

2 Re-read the second paragraph.
   a. How have attitudes to doing voluntary overtime changed since 2003?
   b. Why has this has happened?

3 How do the police officers now decide who is going to work the extra hours?

4 Why does Sgt Bloggs say that being a police officer is not a normal job? Choose two answers from the following statements.
   - Police officers have to work longer hours.
   - The job that police officers do is not appreciated by ordinary people.
   - It is more dangerous, violent and emotionally draining.
   - Police officers have more responsibility than people in most jobs.

5 At the end, Sgt Bloggs says:

'we will get the police force we pay for'

Explain what she means.

What does Sgt Bloggs mean?

6.1 Chapter 6: Viewpoints and issues

📖 Reading skills

Sgt Bloggs chooses her words very carefully and uses a range of language features to support her argument that police officers should be paid more.

1 At the start, she uses some striking adjectives.

  a. What effect does the adjective 'concrete' have in the first paragraph?

  b. Now look at 'whopping' in the same sentence. How does this adjective strengthen her argument?

2 In the second paragraph, she compares the situation in 2003 with the current situation. Bloggs includes an **anecdote** from her own experience as evidence of how things have changed.

  a. Copy and complete the table below to explain the effect of her language choices. The first one has been done for you.

Language to describe 2003	Effect
'putting their hands up'	This image makes the police officers sound like eager school children who are keen to answer a teacher's question. They're full of energy and optimism.
'dealing'	
'doing'	
'covering'	

Language to describe now	Effect
'like pulling teeth'	
'trying'	
'draw straws'	
'gruelling'	

  b. Using the notes from your table, write a paragraph explaining how Sgt Ellie Bloggs uses language to **contrast** the current situation with the past. Use connecting words such as 'whereas' and 'however' to link the contrasting ideas.

Key terms

anecdote a short story about a real person or event

contrast to compare two things to show their differences

Unit 1: Speaking my mind (1)

3 In the fourth paragraph, Sgt Bloggs argues that police work is not normal. To demonstrate her point, she describes what ordinary people do 'in any other job' if they face frightening or challenging situations. She uses a range of language and grammatical choices to make her writing effective. These have been annotated in the paragraph below, along with notes to show how these language features work.

Using these notes and any of your own ideas, explain how Sgt Bloggs uses language effectively in the fourth paragraph to help us understand what it is like to be a frontline police officer.

> **Key terms**
>
> **present tense** used to describe things that are happening now
>
> **rhythm** the pattern made by the 'beats' in language or music
>
> **verb** a word that identifies actions, thoughts, feelings or a state of being

Presenting examples as a list: this is the first in a list of three examples of what police officers encounter.

Repetition of a single word 'if': draws attention to all the awful things that often happen to police officers.

*Using the **present tense** of dramatic **verbs**:* gives an immediate sense of danger.

'In any other job, if someone swears in your face and threatens you, you call a manager or for the police. If there's a fire alarm or bomb alert, you evacuate to safety. If a colleague is attacked and seriously injured, someone else will come to help you and deal with it.'

Directly addressing the reader: makes us take notice.

Repeated sentence structure and punctuation: each sentence is divided in two by a comma, creating a repeated **rhythm**.

! Check your skills

Re-read the fifth paragraph. How does Sgt Bloggs use language effectively to describe what it's like to be a police officer so that we feel sympathy and admiration for them? Comment on:

- sentence structure (e.g. repeated structures and punctuation)
- use of evidence to support views (e.g. examples from a police officer's experience)
- language choices (e.g. lists, repetition, verbs, adjectives).

153

6.2 Chapter 6: Viewpoints and issues

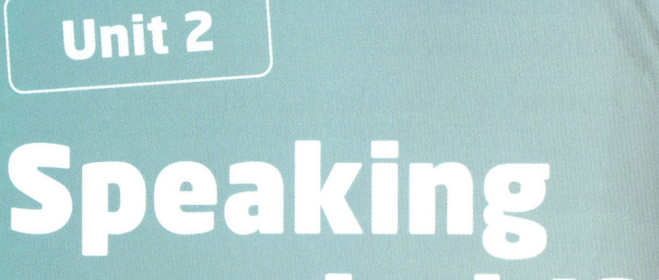

Unit 2

Speaking my mind (2)

In this unit, you will:

- Retrieve information from a letter written in the 19th century.
- Compare the viewpoints of a 19th-century writer with those of a modern writer.
- Learn, understand and practise using new vocabulary.

During the 19th century, most middle- and upper-class families kept servants. These were mostly women (often young girls) who did everything from cooking and cleaning to sewing and mending clothes. They had to live with the families, were poorly paid and had very little time off. Towards the end of the century, however, many of them were able to read and write, and they began to feel that they were not being fairly treated.

In the letter on page 155, taken from a newspaper, an anonymous young maid explains how difficult it was for her to find a new job after being unfairly dismissed.

Ready, set, go!

As you read the letter opposite, think about why the writer might have chosen to put her complaints in a letter to a newspaper.

Unit 2: Speaking my mind (2)

A letter published in the *Western Mail*
371 words

A servant's grievance. Girls ask for protection against tyrannous mistresses

29th November 1892

To the editor of the 'Western Mail'

Sir, – Will you insert a servant's complaints of the way in which the majority of that much-abused **class** are treated? No one seems to heed our long hours or our holidays, which are (**like angels' visits**) few and far between. There seems no other class working at a greater disadvantage. For instance, no servant can expect a **situation** who has not got a good **reference** and a long one from where she last lived. It often happens she has been living with unprincipled people, who think not half so much of their servants as they do of their dumb animals. What is it to them if the girl does not get a situation? She has offended them in some way or other. Perhaps she has had more than her share of work, bad food and other things too numerous to mention, and she has spoken too **plainly** to please them. That, of course, is considered impertinent, for, according to many mistresses' opinion, a servant is a being made **expressly** for them, and she has no rights whatever, and she is told she need not expect a **character**. What are servants to do under these circumstances? They may be out of a situation for months – perhaps something worse. Do the mistresses think we have no **spirit**, and that we must bear quietly the **petty** tyranny they have it in their power to use in a hundred ways?

My two last situations have happened to be places where it is impossible for servants to live, I being the sixth servant in three months, and yet we have nothing and no one to warn us of places of this sort. I think it is a serious matter that our character (I may say our **livelihood**) is at the mercy of such people. Why cannot something be done to benefit servants, as well as other working classes? Servants ought to know what kind of places they are going into, as well as the character of the people they are to live with. – Hoping some nobler pen will take this up, I am, etc.

A servant.

---

mistress – the female head of the household
class – a social group (e.g. servants)
like angels' visits – in the Bible, angels visit humans very rarely
situation – job
reference – a letter from an employer confirming the character and ability of an employee
plainly – honestly
expressly – especially
character – a character reference
spirit – confidence (in this text)
petty – minor or unimportant
livelihood – way of earning money

Many Victorian homes had at least one servant and some had many.

155

6.2 Chapter 6: Viewpoints and issues

⚡ Word power

Re-read the extract on page 155. Pay particular attention to the target words and **phrases** listed below. As you read, think about what the words might mean in this extract.

Your target words and phrases for this section are:

- heed
- unprincipled
- impertinent
- tyranny
- at the mercy

These target words and phrases have been highlighted in blue in the extract on page 155.

> **Key term**
>
> **phrase** a group of words that forms a unit

1. Look up the word 'heed' in the Target word list on pages 174–175. If the mistresses had heeded their complaints, how might servants' lives have changed?

2. Someone who is unprincipled has no morals.

   a. Which of the following would an unprincipled person be most likely to do? Pick two.

   - Mistreat an animal
   - Give generously to charity
   - Travel on a bus without paying

   b. Complete the following sentence.

   Some unprincipled bus passengers...

3. The word 'impertinent' normally applies to a rude way of speaking that breaks social rules. Here are three students speaking to their teacher. Which of them do you think is being impertinent and why?

   - Excuse me, Miss. Can I use the toilet?
   - Sir! Are you married?
   - I'm sorry I'm late, Miss.

4. Tyranny is when someone rules others by force, against their will. A ruler of this sort is called a tyrant. Why do you think that some 19th-century mistresses could be described as tyrants?

Unit 2: Speaking my mind (2)

5. If you are at the mercy of something or someone, you are completely controlled by it or them. Write three sentences, one based on each of the pairs below, describing an event and including the phrase 'at the mercy'.

- slave, master
- cat, mouse
- newly planted trees, icy weather

How would you feel if your life was ruled by a tyrant?

Knowledge and understanding

Look back at the extract on page 155 and answer the following questions.

1. In the first three lines (up to 'far between'), name two complaints that the writer makes about the lives of servants.

2. In the first paragraph, what paper document must a servant have if they are to get a new job?

3. The writer describes what often happens to the servant of a bad employer. Put these events in order (the first has been done for you).

    | 1 | The employer treats the servant badly. |
    | | The employer refuses to give the servant a reference. |
    | | The servant is unable to get a new job and can be out of work for months. |
    | | The servant complains and is accused of being rude and is sacked. |
    | | The servant asks her employer for a reference. |

4. What does the writer suggest at the end of the letter that might help servants avoid bad employers?

6.2 Chapter 6: Viewpoints and issues

Reading skills

1 The letter on page 155 is quite similar to the blog on page 149, even though they were written more than 100 years apart. Both were written anonymously in order to complain about unfair treatment of people who do a difficult job and often go unnoticed.

You are going to compare information from both texts. To help you get started, complete the following tasks.

a. Both the servant and the police officer feel they are badly treated. Some of their complaints are listed below. Decide whether they belong to the police officer or the servant, and write them in the correct column in a table like the one below. Could some go in both columns?

Police officers	19th-century servants

- They have to take on a great deal of responsibility.
- They are not valued by their employers.
- They have no power.
- They have to confront violent people and comfort distressed people.
- They can't speak honestly to their employers.
- They are expected to work too hard.
- They have to take difficult decisions.
- Their complaints are not listened to.

b. To support your decisions, find a quotation from the text for each complaint.

Unit 2: **Speaking my mind (2)**

2 Choose one of the complaints that you think applies to both writers and write a sentence in which you explain the similarities. Include quotations from both texts to support your ideas. You could start:

Both writers feel that…

3 Now choose a different complaint from each column and write a sentence about how the complaints are different. Use the word 'whereas' to link the two ideas.

Tip

You may find the following phrases helpful in your comparison:

- feels that
- thinks that
- explains that
- describes how.

Check your skills

Write a paragraph based on your notes above in which you compare the complaints made by 'Sgt Bloggs' in her blog with those made by 'A Servant' in her letter. Remember to:

- explain the similarities and differences in their complaints
- use connecting words to link and compare your ideas
- support your ideas with quotations and evidence from each text.

It was hard work for a servant in Victorian England.

159

6.3 Chapter 6: Viewpoints and issues

Unit 3

A call to action

In this unit, you will:

- Understand and practise how to structure an **expository essay**.
- Use **counter-argument** to strengthen your argument.
- Learn, understand and practise using new vocabulary.

If you are going to express your point of view effectively in an expository essay, you need to use your knowledge and experience to support your opinions and tailor your writing to suit your audience.

In the article on page 161, which is written in the form of an expository essay, Joanna Cates, a clinical psychologist (who treats people with mental health problems), challenges the idea that smartphones are essential for teenagers. She wants parents to take action.

Key terms

counter-argument when a writer includes an argument that might be put forward by an opponent, in order to argue against it

expository essay an essay in which a writer explores different ideas about a subject, weighing up the evidence for and against these, and setting out their own point of view

Ready, set, go!

As you read the article opposite, notice how the writer supports her opinions with her expert knowledge and her own experiences as a mother.

Unit 3: A call to action

'As parents we need to ask ourselves whether children really need their own smartphones' by Joanna Cates
493 words

Relative to the whole of human history, smartphones have been around for the mere blink of an eye. And yet in that time, we as parents seem to have accepted that having a smartphone is an *essential* part of being a teenager. […]

Okay, fair enough I thought. One day I'll get them a basic mobile phone with a limited amount of credit so they can call me in emergencies.

But now the primary reason for children to own a *smart*phone (because a basic mobile phone just won't cut it these days) seems to have morphed into one about children needing one because otherwise they are going to be cut out of all the 'socialising' that goes on on social media. From the teenagers that I've spoken to, not owning a smartphone is just about the uncoolest thing in the universe. […]

Every day it seems there is another reason as to why we should be concerned about young people's growing dependence on smartphones. These range from the way in which smartphones encourage an obsessive use of social media to the impact that cyberbullying is having on our children's mental health. Research is also starting to emerge about the **negative impact** that owning a smartphone is having on young people's sleep. […]

Owning their own smartphone makes it virtually impossible for parents to really know what sort of material their son or daughter is accessing online. This makes them significantly more vulnerable to **being groomed** and other harmful forces. Parents can set up safeguards and parental controls to some extent but **tech savvy** kids are always going to be one step ahead.

Many people argue that we don't yet have hard evidence that smartphone use by children and teenagers is damaging to them […]. But maybe that's because smartphones haven't been around long enough for much evidence to have yet been produced. In the meantime, are we really planning to experiment with the minds of a generation of young people to see how they cope? […]

For the parents I've spoken to, it's not because they actually want them to have a phone or because they think they need one. It's because if they don't give them one, they will be the only child in their class without one and therefore would feel left out.

So the pressure on parents is enormous. But it is pressure that if parents worked together needn't be there. Because as much as the technology companies try to sell us this technology and our young people pester us to buy it for them, if as parents there was a **collective** agreement that we wouldn't cave in to the pressure then, guess what, the pressure wouldn't be there.

Children want smartphones because *other* children have them […]. If *other* children didn't have them (because *other* parents hadn't bought them for them) we wouldn't find ourselves being bullied into buying them. Only by coming together as parents can we ever hope to turn back the tide.

---

negative impact – bad effect
being groomed – when a criminal persuades a vulnerable person to commit a crime by pretending to be a friend
tech savvy – having an understanding and ability to use technology
collective – all together, acting as one

6.3   Chapter 6: Viewpoints and issues

⚡ **Word power**

Re-read the extract on page 161. Pay particular attention to the target words and phrases listed below. As you read, think about what the words might mean in this extract.

Your target words and phrases for this section are:

- relative
- morphed
- obsessive
- cave in

These target words and phrases have been highlighted in blue in the extract on page 161.

Can you understand this mother's concerns?

1. The phrase 'relative to' is another way of saying 'compared to'. Look at the first sentence of the article and decide which of the following statements are false. The writer is saying that:

   - smartphones were invented recently
   - smartphones are important in human history
   - during most of our history, people haven't used smartphones.

2. Look up the word 'morphed' in the Target word list on pages 174–175.

   a. Use it to complete the following sentence.

   > *On hearing the comment, the usually mild teacher suddenly…*

   b. Write a sentence of your own using the word 'morphed'.

3. If you are obsessive about something, you think about it all the time. Include it in a sentence about each of the people below.

   > He keeps combing his hair and looking in the mirror.

   > She goes to every United match and even owns the away strip.

   > He never misses a *Star Wars* film and collects all the character figurines.

Unit 3: A call to action

4 We can use the **phrasal verb** 'cave in' to describe when someone changes their mind under pressure. Write a short dialogue showing a parent caving in to a child's demands. Remember, at the start, the parent should refuse.

> **Key terms**
>
> **phrasal verb** a verb made up of two words, e.g. *wash up, look after*
>
> **summary** a short text giving just the main points

When will this mother cave in?

Knowledge and understanding

Look back at the extract on page 161 and answer the following questions.

1 Which one of the following statements is an accurate **summary** of the first paragraph?
- Smartphones are bad for your eyes.
- Smartphones have quickly become accepted as essential for teenagers.
- All teenagers have smartphones these days.

2 Re-read the second paragraph. Find two pieces of information that suggest that Cates was reluctant for her children to have smartphones.

3 Re-read the fourth paragraph and find three reasons why smartphones might be bad for teenagers.

4 Why does Cates think that parental safeguards and controls are not effective?

5 In her experience, why are most teenagers given smartphones by their parents?

6 What does Cates want parents to do in order to solve the problem?

163

6.3 Chapter 6: Viewpoints and issues

Writing skills

Cates' argument is well structured and can provide a model for your own writing. To help you understand how the **structure** works, complete the following tasks.

1 The table below summarises all the paragraphs in the article but not in the correct order. Re-read the article and number the statements to show the correct order. The first one has been done for you.

A	It is now accepted that teenagers should have smartphones.	1
B	Let's all take action.	
C	I'm happy for them to have a simple phone for emergency calls.	
D	Owning a smartphone can cause problems for teenagers. They might be bullied online or become addicted.	
E	We don't know yet if smartphones cause long-term damage but it's better to be cautious.	
F	Parents cannot control teenagers' access to online content.	
G	If all parents got together, they could resist the pressure to buy their children smartphones.	
H	Parents only give their children smartphones because they are pressured into it.	
I	Teenagers want phones so they can socialise online and not be seen as uncool.	

2 Now think about the job that each paragraph performs. Which paragraph(s) is an example of each of the jobs below?

- Gives the current situation
- Names the problems
- Presents a counter-argument that is then argued against
- Gives the writer's own experience
- Suggests the solution
- Makes a call to take action

Tip

Some labels will apply to more than one paragraph.

Key term

structure how a text is ordered, the connections made between ideas and themes, and where the writer is directing the reader's focus

Unit 3: A call to action

3 Now it's your turn to plan a well-structured expository essay with the title 'Is handwriting still an important skill for the modern world?' Below are some statements (for and against) to get you started.

> Most adults rarely handwrite anything. Everyone types or texts.

> Clear, legible handwriting tells your reader that you care about presentation.

> You won't always have technology with you, so you need to learn to handwrite.

> Handwriting is more personal. Would you want a word-processed birthday card?

> Learning to write by hand is boring and old-fashioned.

> People such as examiners often judge you unfairly by your handwriting.

Think about how you could use the statements as topics for paragraphs. Plan the structure of your essay by using the order of the bullet points on page 164 to help you. Your first paragraph could look like this:

> In the adult world, very few people write anything by hand anymore. Most writing is now typed on computers and phones.

! Check your skills

Using your plan from the last activity, write the first three paragraphs of your essay. Be sure to use a range of paragraph openers to reflect the different job that each paragraph does.

When you have completed your first draft, check your work for any grammar, spelling and punctuation errors.

6.4 Chapter 6: Viewpoints and issues

Unit 4
A direct appeal

In this unit, you will:
- Explore how a writer's **tone** can engage a reader's sympathy.
- Learn how to use expanded **noun phrases** to construct an effective appeal.
- Learn, understand and practise using new vocabulary.

When we see a person sleeping on the streets, we know that they are homeless and we are often moved to give them money. However, Polly Neate, the chief executive of the housing charity Shelter, wants us to understand that the problem is much bigger than that. In her article on page 167, she explains that homelessness is all around us, often hidden from view.

Ready, set, go!
As you read the article opposite, look at how Neate uses **personal pronouns** to structure her argument.

Key terms

noun a word used to name a place, person, feeling, thing or idea

noun phrase a group of words that has a **noun** as its head or key word. All the words in the group tell us more about the head noun, e.g. *a big muddy puddle* ('puddle' is the head noun).

personal pronoun a word that can be used instead of a name (proper noun), e.g. *I, you, we, us, they, them*

tone how a writer's or speaker's attitude to the subject matter is expressed, e.g. an angry or concerned or polite tone

'Don't assume the only homeless people are those on the streets'
by Polly Neate, the chief executive of the housing charity Shelter
480 words

The arrival of winter so often makes people's minds turn to homelessness. Suddenly the sight of someone shivering on a cold street becomes more disturbing, the heartbreaking image of a child spending Christmas in a **B&B** too vivid to bear.

It's instinctive to want to help. But it's not easy to know how. I've only been at Shelter a couple of months, and already I've been asked several times whether giving money directly to 'homeless people', meaning rough sleepers or people begging on the street, is the 'right thing' to do. It's a challenging question.

There's nothing wrong with giving money away if you want to. But a random act of kindness, with no knowledge of the needs or circumstances of the person concerned, is not going to change anyone's life, or ensure the money goes where it can make most difference or is most needed. The vast majority of 'the homeless' are not visible on the streets but hidden away in hostels, **sofa surfing** or living month-to-month waiting for the chance of a home of their own. Though visible and distressing, rough sleeping is far from the full picture. […]

In parts of London, as many as one in 25 people are recorded as homeless. In Newham or Haringey, even Luton or Brighton, countless homeless people are heading back to a dingy hostel room or B&B every night.

Yet the vast majority go about their lives unseen. They are not begging for money in the streets. In fact, increasingly many homeless people are working, but with stagnant and pitifully low wages, cuts to benefits and rising rents, work these days is by no means a guarantee against homelessness. […]

At Shelter, we make sure this unseen group of people are not forgotten. Our advisers work with them to ensure they get the support they are entitled to and find solutions. […]

You can worry about whether you should give money to someone you see on the street, but that very same day you have probably met another homeless person **hidden in plain sight** – you might be completely unaware that the mother at the school gate or the supermarket cashier has nowhere to call home.

My priority is making sure that Shelter is equipped to deal with this rising crisis. Support from my frontline colleagues transforms lives. Becoming homeless means losing the foundations of your life, the source of stability for you and your children, the sense of safety and security without which we would all struggle. It makes the difference between coping, holding difficulties at bay, and losing control.

Homelessness is dangerous and we can stop it.

To do so we need support. Not random acts of kindness but a deliberate choice to do something about the crisis that so many of our fellow citizens face. The homelessness that is hidden in plain sight because it happens to people just like us.

B&B – short version of 'bed and breakfast', a kind of guest house
sofa surfing – expression used to describe moving from house to house, sleeping on friends' sofas
hidden in plain sight – can be seen but is not recognised or acknowledged

6.4 Chapter 6: Viewpoints and issues

⚡ Word power

Re-read the extract on page 167. Pay particular attention to the target words listed below. As you read, think about what the words might mean in this extract.

Your target words for this section are:

- challenging
- random
- stagnant
- entitled
- stability

These target words have been highlighted in blue in the extract on page 167.

What would you find challenging?

1. The word 'challenging' can describe something that tests your ability or something that is difficult. Look at how the word is used in the extract. Write a sentence using the word 'challenging' to describe something that you feel either tests your ability or is difficult.

2. Look up the word 'random' in the Target word list on pages 174–175, then find it in the article. Explain why giving money to someone in the street could be described as 'a random act of kindness'.

3. We often think of the word 'stagnant' as referring to water in ponds which has become smelly because it doesn't flow. In the article, 'stagnant' is used to describe wages. Which of the following is a **synonym** for this use?

- not increasing
- stale
- smelly

📖 Key term

synonym a word that means the same or almost the same as another word, e.g. 'glad' is a synonym for 'happy'

168

Unit 4: A direct appeal

4 If you are entitled to something, you have a right to it. Imagine that you order an item of clothing online but receive the wrong size. Write a sentence that you could include in your email of complaint, including the word 'entitled'.

5 The **abstract noun** 'stability' comes from the adjective 'stable', which means permanently fixed, not likely to change or fall over. Look at how it is used in the article. What does it mean there? Give an example of this kind of stability.

> **Key term**
>
> **abstract noun** a noun denoting an idea rather than a concrete object, e.g. *truth, danger*

Knowledge and understanding

Look back at the extract on page 167 and answer the following questions.

1 Why might we be more aware of homelessness in the winter?

2 Why is the decision whether to give money to someone begging on the street 'a challenging question'?

Is this the best way to help the homeless?

3 In the third paragraph, why does Neate think giving money to beggars or rough sleepers is not the best way to help the homeless?

4 Why might most of us think that the only homeless people are the ones sleeping rough or begging?

5 Read the following statements.

- All homeless people are unemployed.
- Many homeless people are living in temporary accommodation.
- In London, large numbers of people are homeless.
- Homeless people are usually beggars.

Use information in the article to decide which statements are true.

6 Summarise what the organisation Shelter does, using information from the article.

6.4 Chapter 6: Viewpoints and issues

✏️ Writing skills

1 Polly Neate has a difficult job because she wants to educate us before she can persuade us to donate our money. Telling someone that they are mistaken can be tricky, especially if you want them to donate money to your charity afterwards! In the first three paragraphs, she has to be careful to choose the right polite, understanding tone so as not to insult her readers.

Look at the way that Neate conveys her tone in the extract below.

It's natural to want to help a rough sleeper. We all feel sympathy for them.

> 'It's **instinctive** to want to help. But it's **not easy** **to know how**.'

We all face the same difficult dilemma.

She's going to solve the dilemma and tell us how we can help.

a. Find another example of this tone at the beginning of the third paragraph. Copy it down and explain how it conveys a sympathetic tone.

b. Write your own pair of sentences with a sympathetic tone, suggesting that we should give money to a homeless charity rather than to individual rough sleepers. You might start the first sentence with 'Of course' and the second sentence with 'But'.

Would you realise that a person is homeless?

Unit 4: A direct appeal

2 One of the ways in which Neate persuades us to donate our money is by composing effective expanded noun phrases that draw attention to the homeless.

Re-read the following two paragraphs. Some expanded noun phrases have been highlighted and annotated.

Many homeless people don't live on the street, so they are 'unseen'.

'At Shelter, we make sure this unseen group of people are not forgotten. Our advisers work with them to ensure they get the support they are entitled to and find solutions.

You can worry about whether you should give money to someone you see on the street, but that very same day you have probably met another homeless person hidden in plain sight – you might be completely unaware that the mother at the school gate or the supermarket cashier has nowhere to call home.'

Emphasises that particular time

Gives an example of a someone who looks very ordinary but who might not be helped because they are not obviously homeless

A homeless person might be standing right next to you but you don't know they are homeless and so you don't help them.

Write your own expanded noun phrase to describe each of the following:

a. the 'unseen' homeless

b. rough sleepers.

Remember to keep your tone sympathetic.

! Check your skills

Using the two paragraphs in Activity 2 as a model, write your own paragraph, which could be added to the end of the article, to persuade readers to support Shelter. You could begin like this:

So, the next time that you see a rough sleeper, by all means give them the change in your pocket, but remember that…

- Make sure your tone is sympathetic and understanding.
- Include effective expanded noun phrases that describe rough sleepers and the 'unseen' homeless.

Remember to check your work for grammar, punctuation and spelling errors.

171

6.5 Chapter 6: Viewpoints and issues

Unit 5
Writing assessment

Think back over the extracts you have read in this chapter. Remind yourself of the vocabulary and writing techniques that you have learned. Now it's time for you to put your skills into practice as you complete your own writing task.

Choose one of the writing tasks opposite to complete. Whichever one you select, you should follow the same process below.

1. Plan your ideas. These can be jotted down as bullet points or in a spider diagram.

2. Try to use some of the target words in this chapter, but remember to use them correctly.

3. Write your first draft. Try to make your writing as good as it can be, but remember that you will have the chance to revise and improve it.

4. Edit your draft.
   - Check you have used at least some of the techniques you have learned about.
   - Check your spelling and punctuation.
   - Check that you have created a piece of writing that will keep your reader's attention and put forward your viewpoint strongly.

> **Tip** ✓
> It is often helpful to read your work aloud when you are editing or proofreading.

5. Write a final version ready for assessment.

Unit 5: Writing assessment

Choose **one** of the following writing tasks:

Task A

Write an anonymous letter to a newspaper or a blog post complaining about the way schools currently treat students. Use the following newspaper extract as stimulus.

> Teachers have warned their schools are becoming 'exam factories', turning children off education, as new figures showed 35 pupils a day are now being permanently excluded.
>
> Government statistics from 2015–16 show almost 16 per cent more pupils being banned from school than in the year before.
>
> Children are becoming demoralised by a barrage of tests and a lack of support, the National Union of Teachers (NUT) said, leading to poor behaviour.

← *Do you think the extract above identifies some truths, in your experience?*

Use the anonymous blog on page 149 and the servant's letter on page 155 as models, and include the following:

- evidence from your own experience or typical student experiences
- repeated sentence structures punctuated to create rhythm
- the present tense to make your examples relevant to what happens now
- strong adjectives and verbs
- some figures taken from the stimulus on the left to back up your views.

Task B

Return to Unit 3 and complete the expository essay about the importance of handwriting. Remember to:

- plan each extra paragraph around a clear topic
- start each paragraph differently (include a colloquial opener if you can)
- include a counter-argument so that you can argue against it.

Task C

Using the information and skills that you learned in Unit 4, write a leaflet to be distributed to students in your school entitled 'Should you give money to beggars on the streets?'

Include the following:

- a sympathetic and understanding tone
- effective expanded noun phrases.

Target word list

accent (noun)
   1 a way of pronouncing (speaking) words, especially one associated with a particular country, area, or social class
   2 emphasis on one word, sound or letter in speech
accost (verb) to approach and speak to someone in a challenging way
accustomed (verb) used to
achieve (verb) gain or reach something by effort
act (noun) something done by someone
ambitious (adjective) wanting very much to achieve something, or to do well in life
arranged (verb) put in order or the correct position
at the mercy (phrase) be completely in the power of someone or something

bearings (noun) sense of direction relative to your surroundings
belied (verb) gave a false impression of something
blistering
   1 (adjective) very intense or severe
   2 (verb) producing blisters (bubbles) on the skin or a surface
buckled (verb) collapsed or bent
bulk (noun)
   1 the majority or main part
   2 the shape (usually of something large)
bundle
   1 (verb) to wrap or tie things together
   2 (verb) to put something away hastily and untidily
   3 (noun) a number of things tied or wrapped together

carpeted (verb) covered
cave in (verb) give in to an argument or demand
challenging (adjective) testing or difficult
claimed (verb) said to have a right to something
clamour (noun) a loud confused noise
concrete
   1 (noun) a hard substance used in construction
   2 (adjective) definite or positive
conscience (noun) a person's sense of right and wrong
contemplating (verb) considering
contrary (adjective) opposite
crumpling (verb) crushing into creases

decay (noun) the state or process of rotting
deposited (verb) put something down
desperate (adjective) reckless and ready to do anything
detest (verb) hate
devastate (verb) totally destroy or overwhelm
dour (adjective) stern or gloomy in looks or manner
draping (verb) covering or wrapping loosely
drenched (adjective) made wet through
driven (verb)
   1 taken by car
   2 forced by pressure

dropping (verb) falling by the force of gravity

entail (verb) involve
entitled (adjective) having a right to something
epic (adjective) on a grand or heroic scale

faint (adjective)
   1 pale or weak; not distinct
   2 weak or giddy
felled (verb) knocked or chopped down
flicker (verb) burn or shine unsteadily
focus (noun) something that is a centre of interest or attention

glint
   1 (noun) a brief flash of light
   2 (verb) to shine with a brief flash of light
gravity (noun)
   1 the force that pulls things to Earth
   2 importance or seriousness
gruelling (adjective) extremely tiring or difficult

headlong (adverb) head first, at speed
heed (verb) pay attention to
holding out (verb) waiting
horizon (noun) the line where the Earth and sky seem to meet

impertinent (adjective) rude; not showing respect
incurring (verb) to 'incur' something difficult or unwelcome is to do or say something that makes it happen
inflated (adjective)
   1 filled with gas or air
   2 puffed up with pride
in my blood (phrase) it is natural for you to do something because it's part of your family background
inquiringly (adverb) (also spelled 'enquiringly') in a questioning way
instinctive (adjective) triggered by natural impulse

long (verb) strongly wish
luckless (adjective) unlucky
lush (adjective) growing thickly and strongly

made my… blood boil (phrase) made someone very angry
make a scene (verb) create an angry or noisy outburst
marked (adjective) clearly noticeable
matted (adjective) in a tangled mass
mention (verb) speak or write about something briefly
mingling (verb) mixing
misshapen (adjective) distorted or badly shaped
modest (adjective)
   1 not vain or boastful
   2 moderate in size or amount
   3 not showy or splendid
   4 behaving or dressing decently
morphed (verb) changed in appearance

Target word list

motivated *(adjective)* having a positive, 'can do' attitude

nation *(noun)* a large community of people who live under the same government and share common language, history and customs

obnoxious *(adjective)* extremely unpleasant
obsessive *(adjective)* thinking about something all the time
opportunity *(noun)* a good chance to do a particular thing
originated *(verb)* began
overwhelmed *(verb)* buried or drowned beneath a huge mass

perform *(verb)*
    1 carry out or do something
    2 act publicly for entertainment, such as on a stage
pinning *(verb)* holding someone firmly so they cannot move
precaution *(noun)* something done to prevent future trouble or danger
preliminary *(adjective)* coming before an important action or events
pristine *(adjective)* in its original condition; unspoilt
provoking *(adjective)* rousing interest, anger, excitement or another strong emotion
public *(adjective)* openly; in public

random *(adjective)* without conscious thought or planning
recess *(noun)* a part or space set back from a main line of wall
recovered *(verb)*
    1 to get back a possession that is lost or stolen
    2 to be well again
relative *(adjective)* considered in relation to something else
resolution *(noun)* determination
respectable *(adjective)* honest and decent; acceptable
retrospect *(noun)* a survey of past time
rickety *(adjective)* unstable and likely to collapse

sacrifice *(noun)*
    1 the act of giving up something valued for the sake of something else regarded as more important or worthy
    2 the act of slaughtering an animal or person or giving up a possession as an offering to a god
seedy *(adjective)* unpleasant, shabby or falling apart
sensation *(noun)*
    1 a physical feeling
    2 something of great public interest or excitement
sentinel *(noun)* a guard
separate *(verb)* to keep things apart
simultaneously *(adverb)* at the same time
specifically *(adverb)* in a way that is definite or precise or to do with a particular thing
stability *(noun)* steadiness; security
stagnant *(adjective)*
    1 not flowing
    2 not active or developing

stout *(adjective)* sturdy and thick
stubborn *(adjective)*
    1 strong willed
    2 awkward
    3 difficult
swarming *(verb)* moving around in large numbers

that's big of you *(phrase)* someone has been kind or generous (often used sarcastically)
threadbare *(adjective)* thin and tattered with age
took it in my stride *(phrase)* dealt with something calmly
touched *(adjective)* affected
trial *(noun)*
    1 the process of examining the evidence in a law court to decide whether a person is guilty of a crime
    2 the process of testing something to see how good it is
    3 a test of qualities or ability
    4 an annoying person or thing
tumult *(noun)* loud confused noise; state of chaos
tyranny *(noun)* rule by fear and force

unassuming *(adjective)* modest; not arrogant or pretentious
uncharacteristically *(adverb)* acting in a way that is not typical
undaunted *(adjective)* not discouraged by difficulty or danger
unobtrusively *(adverb)* without attracting attention
unprincipled *(adjective)* acting without good moral principles
uproar *(noun)* an outburst of noise or excitement

vaguely *(adverb)*
    1 in a way that is uncertain, indefinite or unclear
    2 slightly
visibly *(adverb)* in a way that can be seen or perceived clearly
vision *(noun)*
    1 the ability to see
    2 something seen in a dream, trance or as a supernatural image
vocation *(noun)* a strong desire to do or a natural liking for a type of work
voice broke *(verb)* became suddenly deeper at puberty

wandering *(verb)* going about without trying to reach a particular place
whimper *(verb)* cry or whine softly
work ethic *(noun)* principle that hard work has a moral benefit

yanked *(verb)* pulled violently

OXFORD
UNIVERSITY PRESS

Great Clarendon Street, Oxford, OX2 6DP, United Kingdom

Oxford University Press is a department of the University of Oxford.
It furthers the University's objective of excellence in research, scholarship, and education by publishing worldwide. Oxford is a registered trade mark of Oxford University Press in the UK and in certain other countries

© Oxford University Press 2019

The moral rights of the authors have been asserted.

All rights reserved. No part of this publication may be reproduced, stored in a retrieval system, or transmitted, in any form or by any means, without the prior permission in writing of Oxford University Press, or as expressly permitted by law, by licence or under terms agreed with the appropriate reprographics rights organization. Enquiries concerning reproduction outside the scope of the above should be sent to the Rights Department, Oxford University Press, at the address above.

You must not circulate this work in any other form and you must impose this same condition on any acquirer

British Library Cataloguing in Publication Data

Data available

ISBN 978-019-842541-0

10 9 8 7 6 5 4 3 2 1

Printed in Great Britain by Bell and Bain Ltd., Glasgow

Acknowledgements

The authors and publisher would like to thank the following for permission to use photographs and other copyright material:

Cover (clockwise from top): whim_dachs/iStockphoto; Sashkinw/iStockphoto; whitekrechet/123rf; Kostyantyn Ivanyshen/Shutterstock; ryasick/iStockphoto; Linda Bucklin/Shutterstock; GlobalP/iStockphoto; ZargonDesign/iStockphoto. All other photos © Shutterstock, except: **p9**: Antagain/iStockphoto; **p11**: Universal Images Group Editorial/Getty Images; **p12**: Andrea Carroll/iStockphoto; **p13**: Urban Zone/Alamy Stock Photo; **p18**: Michele Falzone/Alamy Stock Photo; **p22**: ROMEO GACAD/Getty Images; **p24**: IuriiSokolov/iStockphoto; **p27**: Goldfinch4ever/iStockphoto; **p31**: BobEdmonson/iStockphoto; **p37**: bastan/iStockphoto; **p40**: vovashevchuk/iStockphoto; **p43**: WesAbrams/iStockphoto; **p44**: Narkorn/iStockphoto; **p46**: ZU_09/iStockphoto; **p49**: Gibon Art/Alamy Stock Photo; **p51**: ErikaMitchell/iStockphoto; **p55**: Anettelinnea/iStockphoto; **p56**: Aniszewski/iStockphoto; **p64**: Diane Labombarbe/iStockphoto; **p74**: LondonPhotos - Homer Sykes/Alamy Stock Photo; **p75**: BananaStock/Getty Images; **p76**: BrianAJackson/iStockphoto; **p79**: monkeybusinessimages/iStockphoto; **p82**: INTERFOTO/Alamy Stock Photo; **p83**: unpict/iStockphoto; **p85**: Everett Collection Inc/Alamy Stock Photo; **p86b**: monkeybusinessimages/iStockphoto; **p91**: Photostage; **p93**: Chris Jackson/Getty Images; **p94**: JayKay57/iStockphoto; **p95**: FamVeld/iStockphoto; **p97**: APCortizasJr/iStockphoto; **p102**: Graeme Baty/Alamy Stock Photo; **p103**: Edward Moss/Alamy Stock Photo; **p106**: VeselovaElena/iStockphoto; **p114**: Henfaes/iStockphoto; **p115**: Some Wonderful Old Things/Alamy Stock Photo; **p119**: Granger Historical Picture Archive/Alamy Stock Photo; **p120**: SBphotos/iStockphoto; **p121**: Rawpixel/iStockphoto; **p124**: Dorling Kindersley ltd/Alamy Stock Photo; p131t: Liderina/iStockphoto; p131m: Poike/iStockphoto; **p134**: Michael Brooke/Alamy Stock Photo; **p136**: DieterMeyrl/iStockphoto; **p141**: Popperfoto/Getty Images; **p145**: Chronicle/Alamy Stock Photo; **p149**: Bettina Strenske/Alamy Stock Photo; **p157**: Walker Art Library/Alamy Stock Photo; **p159**: KGPA Ltd/Alamy Stock Photo; **p168**: Enigma/Alamy Stock Photo; **p170**: Convery flowers/Alamy Stock Photo.

Every effort has been made to contact copyright holders of material reproduced in this book. Any omissions will be rectified in subsequent printings if notice is given to the publisher.

Typeset by Kamae Design

The authors and publisher are grateful for permission to include the following copyright material:

John Agard: 'Crybaby Prime Minister' first published in *Get Back Pimple* (Viking, 1996) from *Half-Caste and other poems* (Hodder Children's Books, 2004), copyright © John Agard 1996, 2004, used by permission of John Agard, c/o Caroline Sheldon Literary Agency Ltd.

Simon Armitage: 'Give' from *Dead Sea Poems* (Faber, 2001), copyright © Simon Armitage 2001, used by permission of Faber & Faber Ltd.

Kate Atkinson: extract from *Life After Life* (Doubleday, 2013), copyright © Kate Atkinson 2013, used by permission of The Random House Group Ltd, and of the author c/o Rogers, Coleridge & White Ltd, 20 Powis Mews, London W11 1JN.

Ellie Bloggs: extract from 'Off with Stress' from www.pcbloggs.blogspot.co.uk, used by permission of the author, Natalie Gaibani.

Ronald Blythe: extract from *Akenfield* (Penguin Classics, 2005), copyright © Ronald Blythe 1969, 1999, used by permission of Penguin Books Ltd.

Charlie Burden: extracts from *Lord Sugar: The Man Who Revolutionised British Business* (John Blake Publishing, 2010), copyright © Charlie Burden 2010, used by permission of the publishers, Kings Road Publishing, Bonnier Books UK.

Darcey Bussell: extract from her story in *Margaret Rooke: Creative Successful Dyslexic: 23 High Achievers Tell Their Story* (JKP, 2016), copyright © Margaret Rooke 2016, used by permission of Jessica Kingsley Publishers Ltd through PLSclear.

Joanna Cates: extract from 'As parents we need to ask ourselves whether children really need their own Smartphones', *Huffington Post*, 11 May 2017, copyright © Joanna Cates 2017, used by permission of the author.

Carol Ann Duffy: 'A Child's Sleep' from *New and Collected Poems for Children* (Faber, 2009), copyright © Carol Ann Duffy 2009, used by permission of the author c/o Rogers, Coleridge & White Ltd, 20 Powis Mews, London W11 1JN.

Kate Ellis: extract from *The Christmas Card List* as published on http://www.thecrimevault.com used by permission of the author, c/o A M Heath & Co Ltd.

Leon Garfield: extract from *Smith* (Puffin Classics, 2014), copyright © Leon Garfield 1967, used by permission of the Estate of Leon Garfield c/o Johnson & Alcock

Morris Gleitzman: extract from *Once* (Puffin, 2005), copyright © Creative Input Pty Ltd 2005, used by permission of Penguin Random House Australia Pty Ltd.

Kiran Millwood Hargrave: extract from *The Island at the End of Everything* (Chicken House, 2017), copyright © Kiran Millwood Hargrave 2017, used by permission of Chicken House Ltd. All rights reserved.

Gerry Harrison (Ed): extracts from *To Fight Alongside Friends: The First World War Diaries of Charlie May* (Collins, 2014), copyright © Gerry Harrison 2014, used by permission of HarperCollins Publishers Ltd.

Anthony Horowitz: extract from *Stormbreaker* (Walker, 2015), text copyright © Stormbreaker Productions Ltd 2000, used by permission of Walker Books Ltd, www.walker.co.uk

Jackie Kay: 'Old Tongue' from *Darling: New and Selected Poems* (Bloodaxe, 2007), copyright © Jackie Kay 2007, used by permission of Bloodaxe Books, www.bloodaxebooks.com.

Polly Neate: extract from 'Don't Assume the only homeless people are those on the streets', *New Statesman*, 9 November 2017, used by permission of New Statesman Ltd.

Terry Pratchett: extract from *A Hat Full of Sky* (Corgi, 2005), copyright © Terry and Lyn Pratchett 2004, used by permission of The Random House Group Ltd.

Jon Sharman: extract from 'Teachers blame obsession with exams as number of pupils being expelled soars', *Independent*, 20 July 2017, copyright © The Independent 2017, used by permission of Independent Digital News and Media/ESI Media.

Martin Stewart: extract from *The Sacrifice Box* (Penguin, 2018), copyright © Martin Stewart 2018, used by permission of Penguin Books Ltd.

Donna Tartt: extract from *The Secret History* (Penguin, 2016), copyright © Donna Tartt 1992, used by permission of Penguin Books Ltd.

Ed Yong: 'A Remote Paradise Island is now a Plastic Junkyard', *The Atlantic*, 15 May 2017, copyright © The Atlantic Media Co, 2017, used by permission of the Atlantic Media Co through Tribune Content Agency. All rights reserved.

Sandra Millers Younger: extract from *The Fire Outside My Window: A survivor tells the true story of California's Epic Cedar Fire* (Globe Pequot Press, 2013), copyright © 2013, used by permission of Globe Pequot Press through Copyright Clearance Center, Inc. All rights reserved.

Although we have made every effort to trace and contact all copyright holders before publication this has not been possible in all cases. If notified, the publisher will rectify any errors or omissions at the earliest opportunity.